MW00827472

STRATEGIC SERIES AUTHOR

PLAN, WRITE AND PUBLISH A SERIES TO
MAXIMIZE READERSHIP & INCOME

CRYSTAL HUNT

CREATIVE ACADEMY FOR WRITERS

Copyright © 2019 by Crystal Hunt

Published by Creative Academy for Writers

All rights reserved.

www.creativeacademyforwriters.com

No part of this book may be reproduced in any form or by any electronic or mechanical means, including information storage and retrieval systems, without written permission from the author, except for the use of brief quotations in a book review.

Disclosure: When there are products or services we like and use ourselves, we've included an affiliate link. It's a win-win, you get something that we love and we get a small amount of money that we will blow on champagne and books.

ISBNs

978-1-926691-98-5 (Mobi)

978-1-926691-99-2 (ePub)

978-1-989662-00-7 (Softcover)

978-1-989662-01-4 (Hardcover)

978-1-989662-02-1 (Audiobook)

Although the author and publisher have made every effort to ensure that the information in this book was correct at publication, the author and publisher do not assume and hereby disclaim any liability to any party for any loss, damage or disruption caused by errors or omissions, whether such errors or omissions result from negligence, accidents or any other cause.

*I wrote this book for **you**.*

I hope it helps you get closer to realizing your writing and publishing dreams, and living your best creative life.

I can't wait to read your series!

xo Crystal

CONTENTS

A note about spelling...

All three of the founding members of The Creative Academy live in Canada, and we made a conscious decision to use Canadian spellings throughout our book series. Because...well...it's who we are, eh?!

A note to our American readers and other friends from around the world... we welcome U in Canada :) Thanks for your willingness to learn new things and play nice with your colourful Canadian neighbours.

While we always appreciate readers letting us know if you find errors in our books, pretty please double check Canadian spellings before you tell us we're wrong.

When we're quoting someone and the quote used American spellings, we left those intact.

xo Crystal, Donna and Eileen

PHILOSOPHY OF THE CREATIVE ACADEMY FOR WRITERS

I come from a really small town on Vancouver Island, on the West Coast of Canada.

Like, the kind of small where I could (and did) read every single book we had in town. I read at least one book a day, and have done that for most of my life. I read while walking, while cooking, on the bus, secretly through more classes than my teachers would want to know about, while in the bath... you get the idea. I read my way through what was on the library shelves at school. And then I moved on to my mom's shelves. And then to the public library. My parents even organized fundraising events to help the school libraries buy more books. (I know, right? Best parents ever.)

But for all that I was positively steeped in stories, I didn't actually know anyone who *wrote* books. It wasn't a job that came up on the list of possible careers. We never had an author come to our school. I don't remember ever hearing of an author visiting our local bookstore. It was way too small for that... and this was of course all in the days before the internet or social media. You couldn't just Google someone and see that they were a real person.

Fortunately, I was shockingly stubborn in my conviction that I was *meant* to tell stories and have believed that since I was in kindergarten. My family was supportive and I moved to the big city at seventeen determined to find my people. Because the books kept appearing on shelves... so I knew that somewhere out there were the people who were writing them.

So I read more, I studied English Literature at university, and I continued filling my notebooks with stories. It was a windy, twisty path towards the life I wanted.

And *damn*, but it was a lonely road sometimes.

But slowly, adventure by adventure, risk by risk, mistake by mistake I learned and met people and collected up a group of people around me who were supportive. Who were writers. Who knew other writers. Who were published authors. And eventually who were the authors that had written so many of the books that had inspired me to become a writer in the first place.

And two of the lovely people I met along the way were Donna Barker and Eileen Cook—now friends, creative collaborators and co-authors! And our goal with The Creative Academy for Writers is really to make sure that you have an easier time finding your people than we had.

Road trips—especially the kinds we writers like to go on—are way more fun with friends.

INTRODUCTION

In this book I will share with you some of the tools and systems I've used in planning my own series, and at each step of the way I'll ask you questions to get you applying that information to your own situation and stories.

But first, a little background.

I didn't originally set out to write a series. When I started jotting ideas in a notebook twenty years ago, I saw the stories all as stand-alones. My focus was on the characters, their lives, their relationships—with the setting in the background.

While I've known since I was five years old that I wanted to write books, I only focused on the storytelling side. I never really thought about the business side. If I thought about it at all, it was some kind of amorphous idea about getting "the call" from some publisher who had naturally recognized the brilliance of my work and was ready to make me famous.

Fast forward to a 25-year-old me, fresh out of a Masters degree in Health Psychology and tired of the academic world. I hadn't written a word of fiction in years, but more than ever I felt like it was my calling. My "backup career" education firmly in place, alongside a supportive partner, and it was time to tackle the whole "being a writer" thing for real.

I started with children's books because I had a few picture book ideas and it seemed like shorter stuff would be an easier starting place. (Cue laughter... it's not. Like, *really* not.) I spent almost a decade steeped in the early (read before it was cool) indie publishing world. Creating 20+ children's books, published through a combination of traditional and indie methods, taught me a ton about the publishing world, about myself, and ultimately about my still very supportive husband.

About five years ago, I switched my focus to writing romance, where I had always felt I was meant to be. It's my first love in reading, and nearly the first thing I'd tried to write—as I started writing my first romance novel at age fifteen.

While attending every meeting and workshop on romance writing that I could find, I also worked my way through 20+ year's worth of notes, storylines, maps, etc. to see how it all fit together. I researched the stats on what books and strategies were making money for indie authors out there in the world.

Everything I read said the best way to establish a dedicated fan-base while also making some cash and setting yourself up for indie publishing success involved writing a series.

I went back to my hard drive (and yes, a couple of binders) full of stories and gave them a close and critical look. I'd basically been setting them all in the same kind of place, and then struggling to try to make it feel like different small island towns.

It wasn't much of a stretch to ask the question: what if they all take place in the *same* small town?

What if, indeed. I set out to bring my town to life, and the *Rivers End Romance* stories were born.

I'm somewhat...er... *organized* in how I operate. I've developed some good resources to help me keep track of things. Well, to keep track of *everything* really. I tried every tool that came across my path and I talked to every writer I met who tackled series, adjusting and revising my own processes to incorporate what I was learning from others.

With each book that I wrote and released, I adapted again to make sure I was fulfilling readers' expectations and learning the business side of things from the data from each book launch.

Added to that mix, I have an amazing support community of friends and fellow writers, many of whom are part of The Creative Academy for Writers (www.creativeacademy-forwriters.com). We give feedback to each other on all kinds of things, share resources, hang out in the early morning hours to get new words on the page every day, participate in mastermind and goal setting chats, and we help spread the word about releases and promos. Most importantly, we celebrate each other's successes!

And you know what? It's working.

In fact, it's working really well.

In the past two years I've managed to write 15 novellas, short stories and full-length romances, in addition to my non-fiction books. And I'm on track to make writing my day job within the next few months.

So here we are. Three years ago, when I went looking for a comprehensive resource to help me organize, create and succeed with writing my book series, I couldn't find one. And when I looked again this past summer, still nothing. So, Donna, Eileen and I decided to package up all the knowledge I've collected and experienced in case other writers were trying to figure out how this "writing a series" business works.

Since you're reading this, I'm guessing you're one of those people.

And now, instead of talking about me... let's talk about you.

HOW TO USE THIS BOOK

You're a grown up (probably) and this is your book. You can do with it whatever the heck you want. But if you *are* open to some suggestions on how to get the most out of the experience, here's what I suggest:

Read it all the way through before you do anything.

Seriously. I know it's long. I wanted you to have everything you need—as much as humanly possible—in one place. If you read through this whole book first, and get a big picture view, when you go back and actually work through the exercises you'll be doing it from a place of knowing what's coming.

Think of it like a *Groundhog Day* situation. If you knew what was coming in your day, you'd make different decisions at certain points, wouldn't you? (I know I sure would.) Planning out the writing and publishing of your series is no different.

Read it all the way through again—then go back and dive into specific areas.

I know, I know. You're crazy busy and you have a billion things to learn and do. But the first time you read it straight through you'll be absorbing everything I collected for you here—getting the framework and all the options settled in your mind. The second time you're reading it should be ALL about YOU. On that read, you will be filtering out anything that's not relevant to your own goals and plans and hopes and dreams and stories, and focusing on specific areas that are relevant to where you're at in the process right now. But if you do that filtering on the first pass, you're going to miss stuff that might turn out to be quite important to your series' success.

There are six main sections in this book.

1. Define your strategy

2. Plan your series

3. Write your series

4. Publish your series

5. Scale up your sales

6. Grow your career

You'll find **Your Turn** exercises mentioned throughout the book.

To make it easier to tell which questions are most relevant to your situation, I've divided them into two sections wherever relevant:

1. Questions for writers working on their first series

2. Questions for writers who are already established series authors

PART I

DEFINE YOUR STRATEGY

1

WHY ARE YOU HERE?

I don't mean in an existential kind of way—although I'd be happy to have that conversation over a pint of cider in a pub!

I mean, why is it that you've purchased this book, and what are you hoping it'll help you accomplish? What are your goals? Your hopes? Your dreams? For both your writing and your life.

Here are some of the reasons why I *think* you might be here:

- You want to quit your day job and be a writer for real, but everyone has told you the only way to do that is to write a series that *everyone* wants to read.
- You love *Lord of the Rings* and want to create your magnum opus; you just don't quite know where to start.
- You're trying to decide between indie or

traditional publishing for your series and you want to know what's involved before you commit to pitch or publish.

- You have a head full of characters who talk to you all the time while you're awake and haunt your dreams, and you're pretty sure the only way to make it stop is to write it all down so their stories get told.
- All of the above. *(I've got my hand up here!)*
- None of the above. (Okay, I'm curious. Seriously, shoot me an email to seriesauthor@creativeacademyforwriters.com and tell me why you're reading this book and what you're hoping to accomplish with your series.)

Regardless of *why* you're writing a series, I hope this book will help you figure out the *how* and *when* pieces of the puzzle.

2

THE KAREFUL APPROACH

What do I mean by KAREful? And no, that's not a spelling mistake, or one of those rogue Canadian spellings I warned you about. I developed this acronym to remind myself of the proper series of phases that need to be part of every project, every new business idea and every single book that I write and publish. It's actually a great acronym to guide the way you do everything in your life. Because being a strategic author isn't just about having a plan, it's also about how you make that plan, and how you carry it out.

KARE stands for:

Knowledge

Action

Reflection

Evolution

Knowledge

Your first step is to stop and make sure you know what you're trying to achieve. Then you're going to do some recon and Google the heck out of whatever you're trying to do and see how other people have already accomplished it.

There are plenty of other authors out there who are killing it—in every area of publishing. You have the opportunity to learn from all of them with just a few keystrokes. Often without spending a single dollar or even putting on pants, as you can do it all from the comfort of your own laptop in the privacy of your own home. Your first step should always be to get as clear a picture as you can about what you're going to be facing in this next step of your writing and publishing journey.

Once you know what you are going to do, how you're going to do it, and who is going to help you if you need it —then you can take action.

If your current goal is to write a murder mystery, you probably want to spend your walking or cooking times listening to podcasts about real life crime, how to write a murder mystery, what makes a good story, etc.

If you've already got published books and your goal is to level up your income from book sales from $500 a month to $5000 a month, then you'll need to watch videos, listen to podcast interviews and read books by folks who have successfully pulled this off and analyse what they did, how they did it, and what kind of timeline seems realistic.

What if you don't know what you don't know and are stuck in the knowledge phase because there is too much to pay attention to? This is when you can reach out to your support networks for help. It might be that you have the resources you need in your own local writer's group, or online through a great writing support community. Or you might do best with a bit of a jump start with a 1:1 coach.

You'll know what your personality needs and your budget supports. Don't be afraid to ask for help. It's much better (and usually cheaper) to get the help in the knowledge stage than it is to get help in the other stages that follow.

Action

This is the part where you do ALL of the things that are needed to move you to your next step. In this phase, to-do lists are your best friend, and time management and budgeting all come into play.

I know, you're a writer and this all sounds very administrative and not in the least bit creative. I can hear you groaning. But being a successful series author requires a lot of hard work and an acknowledgement that **this is a business**—at which you will work *very hard*. Maybe I don't have to tell you that, because just the fact that you're reading this book tells me you get that there's more to this whole journey than just having a great idea and a laptop.

Reflection

Once you've done a thing, you need to pause and reflect on whether or not it worked, and then adjust your process accordingly so that every single stage, every single book, every single publication cycle is better than the last. Even if the changes you're making save you only a couple minutes, a few dollars, or get you a handful more readers —those changes are cumulative and will add up to very noticeable improvements over time.

I firmly believe that it is this stage that is most often missed by authors. Maybe because when we're dealing with creative works that are close to our hearts, it can be hard to acknowledge that they could have been better in some way.

But you have an advantage over the single title author. What you are building is much bigger than just one book. You are writing a **series**. And that means that every flaw you identify in your process, every weakness in your storytelling ability, every opportunity to connect with a reader that is missed with one book and **corrected**, will ripple out and positively impact every single future book you write.

This is the true power of writing a series. You're not starting over from scratch with every book. You're building on the successes of the previous book, and growing your skills and expertise around the world you've created.

Evolution

The final phase is about making changes and adjustments based on what you've learned in the Reflection stage. If the data showed you that not enough people are downloading book one in your series, then you know you need to change something about your process. It might be that you need to advertise, or make your first book in the series free, or that you need a better cover or blurb to entice people to download it. Maybe you need to do more editing or revisit some craft workshops. But you know that when you reflected on the results, they were not what you wanted. This is your chance to make a course correction that will set you up for better success with future books.

After each book I write, I look back at the comments from my editor in both the developmental editorial letter and the copyediting stage, and ask:

> Is there anything I can change about my process to avoid receiving the same comments on my next book?

If the issue is around the character's internal conflict not being clear enough, that would lead me back to the Knowledge stage where I would do some research about how to better develop my character's backstory and emotional depth (hint: read *Build Better Characters: The psychology of backstory & how to use it in your writing to hook readers* by Eileen Cook if you need help with this) and then be ready to take action with a new tool or awareness as part of my process going forward on the next book. And I think every editorial letter I've ever gotten has suggested upping the conflict.

I've found that making this reflection process a habit is one of the most effective and most efficient ways to make consistent, incremental improvements in every area of my life—not just writing and publishing. But for now, practice by using the KAREful approach as you work through this book, and whatever project you're currently tackling.

3

THE FOUR QUESTIONS OF THE APOCALYPSE

The four questions

As you go through this book and begin applying the ideas in it to the series you're writing, you will be developing all kinds of processes, using tools and creating reference materials to help you navigate around in the world you're building.

If you don't have systems in place yet, and have no idea what systems or tools you'll need, fear not. All will become clear in the next few chapters.

Before you commit to the tools and systems you're going to use, take a second to think about the following four things—and make these things a goal and a filter for every decision you make from here on out.

1. Is it portable?

Life happens. Often, and sometimes with little warning. When you consider a system or tool, think about how easy it is to move.

Anyone who knows me, is aware how truly horrific my sense of direction is. Since my stories all take place in one town, I need to reference a map of the town when characters are moving to and fro so I can keep it all straight. While I seriously wanted to paint my town map onto my office wall, I didn't want to be tied to a specific location or be without the map when I travel. So, I created the map digitally and have a large printout pinned to my wall.

Whenever you're setting up a system to support your writing ask yourself:

• Is it portable? Can you take it with you if you need/want to travel?

• What happens if your house is sold or there is a fire?

• Can you fit what you need in a briefcase or backpack so you have everything you need when you're working on your story away from your regular writing space?

2. Is it flexible?

I don't mean are the tools literally bendable. What I mean is can your systems expand with your needs as you change and grow as an author?

- Will the systems work reasonably well with stories of different lengths?

- If you write a different type of story?

- Whether you have five stories, or fifty?

3. Is it sustainable?

It's great to have all these tools for tracking things, and building out your world, and databases filled with characters. But if you're not using them, and using them consistently, then you've just created a massive black hole of procrastination and time suckage.

You need systems that will grow with you and are adaptable to fit your needs as you evolve as an author. They also need to be financially sustainable.

- Can you support the tools you're paying for?

- Are they widely enough used that they're likely to still be supported in five years?

- Can you afford to use the tools (or service, like editor/cover designer) on every single book you write?

4. Is it backed up?

Yeah, we all know we *should* have backups of everything. Lots of people even do create backups from time-to-time. But you want to know that you're never going to lose more than an hour's work, and ideally not even that if you can help it. You want to make sure that whatever system you're using, it's backed up in a way that happens frequently, automatically, and is stored somewhere you are not.

What if your laptop gets dropped? Or that backpack with a notebook full of all your reference materials is stolen? Or a water main bursts outside your house and completely destroys your home? Or your hard drive literally catches on fire (she says while nodding sagely and cringing at the gut wrenching panic she can still feel, as none of these are hypotheticals).

You are going to learn from my misadventures. You are going to be **smart**. And **savvy**. And **organized**. And absolutely **prepared to succeed**. Because you have me as your cautionary tale.

You are a **strategic series author,** my friend. And you are going to rock this.

4

START WHERE YOU ARE

It's important to know where you're starting from and be aware of your own abilities, experience and inclinations when it comes to writing your series.

In each of the following sections, you'll be asked some questions at the end. Be honest when you answer them. The more honest you are, the more likely you are to be successful.

Don't beat yourself up if you're partway into writing a series and you haven't been doing these things. It doesn't mean you need to scrap everything and start again. We are all learning with every book that we write.

Use what you've learned during those first books to help you figure out what systems will be most useful for you, and then "backtrack" a little and catch yourself up.

You can enter plenty of info retroactively. The important part is to make sure everything gets included, and that moving forward you have all your details tracked.

You can even revise and relaunch a book or whole series if you decide you need a fresh start to level up.

I love the expression, "Meet yourself where you are." And that's just what you're going to do.

First, let's figure out where you are.

Your Turn

This exercise will help you identify general areas where you are strong, and what you need to develop. This exercise focuses on your general skills, knowledge and habits as a writer. Then we'll focus in on various areas as they relate to writing and publishing a series as we work through the coming sections.

Complete the free Writer's Self Evaluation which you can download from:

creativeacademyforwriters.com/resources/strategicseriesauthor.

Reflect on the areas where you are strongest, and where you have some room for growth and improvement. Keep these in mind as you set your specific goals in the coming sections.

5

MANAGE YOUR BUSINESS

I know, I know. I used the B word. But let's be honest… when you go from wanting to write one book to becoming someone who wants to write a series of books, you're diving into a pond filled with authors who are *serious* about the business of writing books (and *extremely serious* about the business of publishing if they're indie).

And no matter how creative you are, ultimately you are running a **business**. Whether you're going the traditional publishing route or indie—the second you exchange money for your time and your words, you're in business.

You'll need systems for each of the stages of the writing and publishing process, and we're going to tackle these, section by section throughout the book. The ones below are things that are critical to the administration side of your business, as well as the overall management of your writing projects.

Manage your finances

You will need a bank account to receive your royalties—ideally one that is separate from your personal finances. You will need somewhere to store digital and physical receipts, and some kind of system for tracking income and expenses so you can accurately and confidently do your taxes at the end of each year. The type of tools you choose for this will depend on your comfort with technology and the size and complexity of your author business.

If you have an accountant or bookkeeper already, make sure to ask them about their preferences for how they would like to receive the information from you. This will save you time and money!

Tools/components

- separate or sub-account of your regular bank account where royalties are deposited
- a file folder for physical receipts
- a Dropbox/Google drive folder for digital receipts
- a spreadsheet or free cloud accounting program/app for tracking income and expenses (Wave Accounting is a good app and free at the time of writing. I used this until I incorporated my company. Quickbooks Online is a paid tool, and is what my accountant works with, so I now use that.)

Your Turn

- Do you have a system to track your income and expenses for your writing business?
- If yes, and it includes all the components you need, then skip to the next section.
- If not, review the list above and decide what tools you will use to keep track of the income and expenses as your author business grows with each new release.

Manage your time

You will want some kind of calendar program, day planner or wall calendar to help you organize your time. This should be used for keeping track of appointments, release dates, interviews, promotions and anything else that is **a time-specific and concrete commitment**.

With each consecutive book you write and release in your series, you will have more time commitments for promotion, more scheduled things to manage (KDP enrolment periods, $0.99 promotions, podcast interviews to promote your latest release, BookBub features...you get the idea!)

Digital is often easier to make changes in, more portable and more convenient for collaboration, but if you're not a fan of technological solutions, the most important thing is that you will *use* whatever system you have. Fancy is not the priority here. Effectiveness and consistency of use is the most important aspect of a good calendar tool. And that it is portable.

Tools/components

- Day planner, wall calendar or whiteboard calendar can be used if you want an offline solution.
- **Google Calendar** and **iCal** (for Mac users) are great tools for keeping track of personal, book-related and publishing commitments. Both Google Calendar and iCal can be shared with other people so you can keep *all* your calendars in one place and easily collaborate with others. Both are free. And both integrate with most appointment booking tools.

Your Turn

- Do you already have a calendar program you use that you love and is fulfilling all your needs? If you do, give yourself a pat on the back and skip ahead to the next section.
- If not, choose a calendar tool you will use to keep track of appointments and time-bound commitments.
- Enter recurring commitments, appointments and meetings. Block the time for your writer's group meetings, mastermind groups and coffee with your critique partner. Put in scheduled promotion dates

for existing books, deadlines for drafts and artist dates to recharge…in other words, enter every date you've got written down on paper or are holding in your head.

Manage your tasks

You'll need some kind of system to manage your to-do lists. Once you're juggling multiple books this can get confusing and overwhelming fast—if you don't have a way to keep these tasks organized.

Tools/components

- A **notebook** or **whiteboard** beside your desk are great options for keeping your lists handy and your priority tasks front and centre. They're not always portable or easy to keep updated without lots of rewriting though (remember those four questions of the apocalypse?).
- **Asana** is the free, cloud-based tool that works on any operating system that I use to track projects and tasks. I'm not gonna lie—the fact that you can turn on "Celebrations" and get animated unicorns and other magical creatures randomly fly across the screen when you complete tasks is up there on the list of why I've been using it for years now. Asana also has an app so you can add tasks from your phone or your computer.
- **Things** (Mac only, sorry PC peeps) is the other program I love. This is a paid app, but the interface is gloriously clean and intuitive. There's a device

app as well, and you don't have to be online for the computer version to work. No unicorns, sadly. But otherwise it rocks.

Your Turn

- What system and/or tool(s) will you use to manage your tasks and to-do lists?

6

ORGANIZE YOUR ASSETS

Even if you're a first time author, it's likely that you've made some progress on your project before you picked up this book. And for you well-established authors, you may have a whole wealth of creative and business assets out there.

Now, I'm not talking about the fancy car or the beach house in the islands you may have picked up with that last royalty cheque (dream big peeps). In this case I'm talking about your **creative** assets.

This includes things like:

- existing tracking tools
- old draft manuscripts
- your laid out book files
- audiobook files
- character sketches
- Scrivener files

- promotional images
- lists of past reviews
- ISBN records
- and on and on the list could go.

Likely, the longer you've been writing and publishing, the bigger the jumble all of this is. I've been doing this author business thing for fifteen years: I'm working on book number 37 for me, and about 250 counting client and student books I've helped produce.

Most of these books were finished under tight deadlines, with last-minute changes and many have been published in multiple formats, some with multiple editions over time.

You sweating yet? Yeah, me too. Or at least I sweat when I think about going back through that older stuff. The stuff I set up **before** I had a system.

You see, it used to be just me working on most things. For years I ran a one woman show. Then the publishing and consulting side grew, and I introduced a business partner (my super organized husband) and then added many, many contractors to my team, and then more business partners.

And what we discovered was that my brain works astonishingly well in the moment. I can keep everything sorted out, and be on top of stuff, and manage versions and file locations and keep it all good and clean and right and wonderful.

But when it came to having someone else step in to pick up where I left off? Disaster.

And when I had to go back in my files and pull out a project I hadn't worked on in months or years to update those book files? Yeah, there's the cold sweat we talked about earlier. The few times I've had to do this have been *educational* (because I promised myself I wouldn't swear in this book). These *educational* moments taught me several important lessons. And in fact, anyone who's read books on decluttering (yes, it *is* life-changing magic!) might recognize some of these tips. They apply to your physical stuff as well as your digital stuff.

Here are a few survival tips:

- You *must* have a clear system for naming and organizing files.
- You *must* use your system 105% of the time.
- You *must* have the rules of your system written down, so that when you take a break you don't forget what your system was and why you were doing things that way.

There is a proper way to name files so they will organize themselves. A way that will save you if you accidentally slip-up and store your files in two folders (or nine folders at different levels on your desktop inside other folders called "To Be Filed" *cough*), so that when you pull them all back into one organized folder several months or years down the line, there is order and sense to them. You know, when your computer finally stops working and *motivates* you to clean up your desktop.

The rules of file naming

Having tried many different varieties of file naming, this is the one that has proven the most effective for organizing all my book files:

Project_Phase_Version_Year-Month-Day_Person.extension

And if you have multiple pen names, you may want to add the pen name on there, too.

Why this? You need a system that will auto-sort your files to group all the same kinds of things together automatically, allow you to follow your workflow and easily see, at a glance, what the most current files are.

If you name your files consistently this will save you time, money and frustration. I guarantee you will swear less, be less tempted to drink, make fewer mistakes and overall will have much more time and energy for your writing. Which at the end of the day, is what this is all about.

Here's a sample of a file structure you would see in one of my project folders in Dropbox, so you can see it in action.

- CJHunt-CHARMED-Draft-V1-2019-05-27.scriv
- CJHunt-CHARMED-Draft-V2-2019-05-30.scriv
- CJHunt-CHARMED-Draft-V2-2019-06-15-ABdevedits.scriv
- CJHunt-CHARMED-Draft-V3-2019-06-15-CJrewrite.scriv
- CJHunt-CHARMED-Draft-V3-2019-06-15.doc
- CJHunt-CHARMED-Draft-V3-2019-06-23-ABcopyedits.doc

- CJHunt-CHARMED-Draft-V4-2019-06-26-CJcopyedits.doc
- CJHunt-CHARMED-Draft-V4-2019-06-29-BetaReaders.doc
- CJHunt-CHARMED-Draft-V5-2019-07-02-CJBetaEdits.doc
- CJHunt-CHARMED-Draft-V5-2019-07-04-ARCTeam.vellum
- *Then there's an* ADVANCE READER COPY *folder that contains ePub, Mobi & PDF versions that go out to my ARC Team/Review Crew.*
- CJHunt-CHARMED-Draft-V6-2019-07-04.vellum
- CJHunt-CHARMED-Draft-V6-2019-07-04-ABProof.PDF
- CJHunt-CHARMED-Final-V7-2019-07-04.vellum
- *Then there's a* READY FOR UPLOAD *folder that contains ePub, Mobi & PDF versions that get uploaded to my publishing outlets.*

And if I make changes to the files after that initial publication (which I always do, to update the **Also By** page, or my back matter or sample when new books come out) then you'd find:

- CJHunt-CHARMED-Final-V8-Revisions-2019-09-14.vellum

Your Turn

- Decide on a file naming convention that you will stick to.
- Create a folder structure on your computer or in your cloud service
- Gather all your book and series related files from where they are are currently living and put them into your new system. Rename them as required.

7
CLARIFY YOUR PURPOSE

Setting goals is an important part of any successful series author's strategy.

How will you define success?

I alluded to it earlier, but **why** do you want to publish a series? What is it that motivates you to show up with your laptop and get those words on the page day after day? How will you know when you are successful?

There are three key pieces of information that you need to know about before you set off on this journey. Your **what**, your **why** and your **how**.

Your WHAT

The first thing you need to determine is **what** you actually want to accomplish. If you don't know what you're trying to achieve or complete then you'll have a very, very hard time planning to get there.

Let's look at three examples to make this really clear.

- Jake wants to be a successful fantasy series author.
- Eloise wants to have a five book non-fiction series traditionally published.
- Tanisha wants to indie publish a seven book series of historical romance novels.

What do you notice about these authors' answers to the question: What do you want to accomplish?

Both Eloise and Tanisha had very specific **what** statements that lend themselves easily to further actions for the Knowledge stage (the K in KAREful), right?

Once Tanisha has identified what she wants to accomplish, she can break this statement down and start gathering knowledge on:

- Indie publishing
- Self-publishing a series
- Writing romance
- Types of series in romance
- Historical romance conventions / trends
- Sales figures in sub-genres of historical romance
- And on and on it goes…

So Jake, wants to be a successful fantasy series author… now what? It stands to reason he'll want to write the best fantasy books that he can, but how will he know when he's "successful?" Will he have any idea when he's achieved his goal? Not so much.

A better **what** statement for Jake might be:

Jake wants to earn $10,000 per month from royalties on his fantasy series.

Or

Jake wants to get his series of fantasy books onto the shelves at brick and mortar bookstores in each province across Canada so he can do in-person signing events.

Or

Jake wants an active mailing list with more than 10,000 subscribers so that each time he launches a new book in his series he can expect to sell 1000 units on launch day just from readers on his list.

You can see how all of these statements fit the original "Jake wants to be a successful fantasy series author." But the alternates give us a much clearer picture of where Jake is headed, which gives us clues about how to get from here to there and what areas he needs to focus on to do that.

Your Turn

- What do you want to achieve with your series? Try to craft at least 3-5 very specific goal statements.

Your WHY

If you embark on your writing and publishing journey without a specific goal that makes it clear what you want to accomplish, it's like setting off on a road trip without a destination in mind, and without any maps or a GPS. Does that mean your trip will be a waste of time? Not necessarily. Depends on **why** you're setting off on that road trip. Your **why** is going to be the driving force behind most of the decisions you make on the way to your **what**.

Let's go back to Eloise for a minute. Eloise wants to have a five-book non-fiction series traditionally published. There are many possible reasons why Eloise wants this. They might include any one or more of these reasons:

- To get an advance big enough to pay off her student loans.
- To build her career to the point where she gets to appear at conferences and events alongside her favourite authors.
- To focus just on writing and not have to deal with all the business side of things the same way she would if she decided to indie publish the books.
- Because she doesn't have the funds to indie publish them properly and she's not willing to compromise on the quality of the books.
- So that her family finally take her writing seriously.
- To share her knowledge, experiences and stories with the world.

You can see how these different **whys** might influence different choices along Eloise's writing and publishing journey.

Extra credit: I found the book *Start With Why* by Simon Sinek to be a great read if you're looking for more help to clarify your **why**.

SMART goals vs SMARTER goals

You might be familiar with the term SMART goals; it's been used for decades in corporate and educational settings. It's basically a list of things you check your goal statement against to make sure it's the most useful. There are many different versions of this acronym, but according to this idea, you want goals that are:

Specific

Measurable

Achievable or **A**ctionable

Results-oriented

Time-bound

Vs SMARTER goals which add:

Exciting

Risky or **R**ewarded

. . .

Personally, I like SMARTER-R goals the best (using both Risky *and* Rewarded). Especially in the strategic series author world, the power of making sure what you're writing is **rewarded** as well as **exciting** is really important. It's likely going to take you years (or sometimes even decades) to achieve those really big overarching goals (like make the *USA Today* bestseller list, for example). I also love **risky** because in committing to writing a series, you've got to be striving for something big enough and exciting enough to make sticking with it worthwhile.

If there's no risk in a story, if the character has nothing to lose in the scene or the book, the story's not that engaging, right? Same thing applies to life. Research backs it up.

Now, that doesn't mean mortgaging your house to pay for indie publishing your books. That's not a *good* kind of risk.

But publicly declaring that your goal is to hit a best-seller list? Or write fifteen books in your series in the next five years? Or double your monthly royalty income with each book in a series that you release? That's risky in a "not dangerous to your basic wellbeing or family's financial stability" kind of way. And don't worry, if that seems totally overwhelming you can start with something that's a small risk like telling the other folks in your writer's group your goal to write and publish a three-book series (or whatever). You can work up to telling the rest of the world.

Your Turn

- For each statement you wrote down in the previous section about **what** you want to achieve as a strategic series author, write down **why** you want to achieve that particular goal.

8
BRAINSTORM NEXT STEPS

Now that you've identified what you want and why you want it, it's time to look at **how** you're going to get it. We will identify some specific steps in the process you need to take, and then we're going to look at different kinds of resources you have access to that are going to help you with those next steps.

How do you figure out what your next steps are?

Let's use Eloise as an example. She wants to have a five book non-fiction series traditionally published.

Once Eloise has identified what she wants to accomplish, she can break this statement down and start gathering knowledge on:

- Traditional publishing
- How to pitch a non-fiction book

- Writing from a book proposal
- Writing non-fiction
- Which publishers are interested in books like the ones she's thinking of
- Trends in length of book for non-fiction for the publishers she's targeting
- How to get an agent for non-fiction
- And the list goes on…

It's much easier to confidently move forward on your writing and publishing journey when you know what resources you have and need.

Your Turn

Review your responses on the Writer's Self Evaluation at:

https://creativeacademyforwriters.com/resources/strate-gicseriesauthor/and think about that information in the context of what you need to do next to move your **series** project forward. Which phase are you in right now?

Knowledge: What areas do you need to learn more about before you're ready for your next action stage? Brainstorm a list.

Action: Are you ready to take action on your series in some way? Brainstorm a list of actions you know you need to take next. If you're stuck, go back to the Knowledge stage and brainstorm a list of possible people, organizations or resources you could use to help you make a list of next actions.

Reflection: If you're in the reflection stage of your project ask yourself: What's working? What's not working? Draw a line down the middle of a piece of scrap paper. On the left, make a list of anything that isn't working for you, or could be better. On the right make a list of everything that is working great. What do you need to do in order to move the items on the left over to the right hand column?

Evolution: Make the changes you identified in your reflection stage, and go back into the Knowledge/Action phases.

9

INVENTORY YOUR TOOLS

I do love me some writing tools. I'm a notebook addict, a software junkie and a lifelong collector of writing craft books. And, I take ALL. THE. COURSES. When I picture heaven it's a beautiful place where the air is thick with words and the puffy white clouds are raining coloured Post-It Notes and shiny new markers.

This category of tools also includes things like laptops, subscriptions to services that help with your writing, memberships to groups that provide education and discounts on other products… all are tools in your writerly toolkit.

But some tools are more useful than others. Some types of software are a great investment, while others languish on your hard drive and do nothing but make you feel regret when you look at them. Some 'free' tools aren't supported long term and end up costing you time and money when you have to transition to something new.

The strategic series author weighs their tool purchases before making them and chooses wisely. You'll be learning about some of my favourites and why I love them later in this book, and we'll look at different options for every budget.

For now, you need to take stock of what you already have and how much those tools are costing current and future you. Then we'll look at things to add or substitute.

Your Turn

You're going to make an inventory of the tools you have in your writing and publishing toolkit. You can do this on a notebook page or in your laptop, or if you'd like to use our ready-to-use spreadsheet, you can download it from creativeacademyforwriters.com/resources/strategic-seriesauthor or set it up as a Google Sheet if you want to have cloud access from any computer.

- Make a list of all the writing tools you know you have, what stage of the writing and publishing process they are used for (planning, writing, editing, publishing, promoting, or business/admin), and what specifically they are for (for example ProWritingAid is used for editing manuscripts before I send it to my editor for copyediting).

- Note whether each tool is free or paid.

- For tools you pay for, note whether it was a one-time fee, is a monthly subscription, or is renewed annually.

- For tools you pay monthly or annually to keep, write down both the amount you pay and the renewal date.

- Highlight or put a star beside the tools you actively use.

- Cross out or put an 'X' beside the tools you no longer use.

- Circle the tools that you forgot you even had.

You don't have to do anything with this information yet… but it'll serve as a starting place for you. Whenever I mention a different tool, you'll be able to easily see if you have something else that does the same job already, or if you can upgrade or downgrade that line item in your budget by switching to something different.

10

STRETCH YOUR LEGS

Still with me? I'm absolutely thrilled by that. The fact that you didn't skip the first section and dive right into the writing and publishing stuff that follows means you're seriously invested in setting yourself up for success, not just looking for that ever elusive quick and easy fix.

You, strategic series author, are much more likely to be successful.

You, strategic series author, are thorough, you're taking advantage of every bit of information that comes your way, you're planning and you're in it to win it.

Awesome.

Now, take a quick stretch break, give yourself a pat on the back, or a gold star on your habit chart or whatever it is that you do to reward yourself for a job well done.

Then refill your water and get ready to dive deep into the actual planning of your series.

PART II

PLAN YOUR SERIES

UNDERSTAND SERIES LABELS

What counts as a series?

How many books do you have to have that are connected before you can call it a series? We're back to that "how long is a piece of string?" question. It's just as long as it needs to be. But for the purposes of us all being on the same page as we work through the following exercises and case studies, let's define a few terms first so that I know, that *you* know what I'm referring to when I use these terms.

Series

According to Wikipedia, *"a book series is a sequence of books having certain characteristics in common that are formally identified together as a group. Book series can be organized in different ways."* There's no specific required number of books that must occur in a series... other than more than one.

Duet/Duology

Some folks on the internet argue that this is a made up thing. That if you have two books, you have a book and its sequel. But that feels like splitting hairs. If there are two books that are formally identified together as a pair (or group) then I think it's reasonable to use the terms duet and/or duology, and that you approach them with many of the same strategies that you would for a series with more titles in it.

Trilogy

Three books that go together and are connected in some way. Again, this seems pretty straightforward and in line with Wikipedia's definition. As humans, we like things grouped in threes. Groups of three books are no exception to that rule. And this has the added benefit of only having to maintain your interest, as the writer, through three books, being able to "complete" the story and character arcs relatively quickly, and being something readers can tear through in a compact period of time (which translates to high read-through).

Numbered series

These stories share characters and a genre, and usually a world—but there are generally few or no references to past events. And character change isn't really common in these books.

Some of the most famous numbered series are the *Nancy Drew* and *Hardy Boys* books. *Goosebumps* by R.L. Stine is another great example. I absolutely loved all of those series and devoured the books in them. This kind of series can be read in any order, with readers jumping in and out anywhere they want.

Sometimes books in a numbered series are put together by book packagers with titles written by multiple authors under one pen name. Imagine my dismay when I discovered in my early 20's that I would never get to meet Carolyn Keene, the author of the *Nancy Drew* mysteries! But learning that Carolyn Keene was actually many authors, sure did explain the variances I had noticed as a young reader in the writing style and details from book to book.

Mini-series

I'm not gonna lie, when it comes to the book world this may be a term that doesn't officially exist. We use it in TV and movies to describe a program that tells a story in a predetermined, limited number of episodes. But in the context of *this* book, I have used it to describe smaller, self-contained book series that are also part of a larger series.

For example, all of the stories I write are set in a town called Rivers End. So technically, every single book I have fits into the larger *Rivers End Romance* series.

But within that larger series are smaller mini-series that focus on a business, a family, a specific series of events... or whatever else seemed interesting enough to me at the time. And there are characters that act as connecting threads from one mini-series to the next. We'll get into the why of that later in this book.

Serialized story

Some series are really serialized stories. This is when the entire series may share a single story arc, or is really one long book broken down into parts. These may be full length pieces like Stephen King's *Dark Tower* series, or *The Lord of the The Rings* by Tolkien. Or they can be stories broken into chapters, parts or volumes. Romance author H.M. Ward is a master of this type of series.

12

IDENTIFY SERIES TYPES

There are many different types of threads that can tie a series together. You can have stories that take place in the same world, feature the same characters, or that are all connected by the same events. I've put together a list of the most common types with some explanation and examples to help you decide which of these aspects your own series will include.

And, if you are one of those authors who are already a few books deep in your series, you can still do these exercises based on identifying what you've got now and how you're going to build out from here.

Connected by setting

1. Share a world

You have a fantasy world and all the books take place there. Think of the Marvel or DC comic book universes.

You have different superhero characters in different settings, but they share a *world*. That's the primary connecting thread.

2. Share a setting

Some series are connected because they take place in the same setting, like a town or city. A great example is Louise Penny's *Chief Inspector Gamache Mystery* series which (mostly) all take place in the fictional town of Three Pines. As the series title suggests, in this case, each story also shares one main character, the police officer in charge of identifying a murderer. This type of series can also be written by multiple authors—like the *Mail Order Brides* historical romance stories.

3. Share a specific location

Similar to books that are connected by setting but even more specifically, by the same actual location, such as an apartment building or a spaceship, or a haunted house at different times over history. The stories may or may not also be connected by the people who live and work in the specific location. For example, all five stories in romance author Cora Seton's *Brides of Chance Creek* series take place on the family's ranch in Chance Creek.

Connected by an object

This kind of series has an object as the central connecting thread. *Sisterhood of the Traveling Pants* is a good example—it's the pants that weave together the stories of the four girls, not just in one book but through all the books in the series. Even when the girls grow apart and no longer share a location or the events of their daily lives, the pants connect them—and the stories—into a series that readers want to read all the books in.

Connected by characters

1. Share a single character

Some series follow a single character and that is the connecting thread. This featured character has adventures one after the other and we become very attached to the character regardless of what setting they're in. Lee Child's *Jack Reacher* books are a great example. For most of the books, Reacher is the only thing that's familiar. The locations and all the other characters are often different from book to book. Kathy Reichs is another example with her *Temperance Brennan* books (which are the inspiration behind the TV series *Bones*). And then there's the *Harry Potter* series, of course.

2. Share a group of characters

Series can be connected by a group of characters. Nora Roberts' *Gallaghers of Ardmore* trilogy is connected by the family of three siblings, and each book is from a different point of view.

Connected by timeline or event

Sometimes a series is based around a single event or a series of events. We follow different characters or groups of characters in the different stories, but the piece that ties them all together is the events happening. *A Song of Ice and*

Fire series by George R.R. Martin is an example of a series connected by the events happening in the story.

Connected by story arc

Some series are really a very long story that has been broken into multiple parts—these are the serialized stories I spoke about in the previous chapter.

Others?

Are there other kinds I haven't mentioned here? Probably. If you've got an idea of something I should add in future editions of this book please email me at seriesauthor@creativeacademyforwriters.com and let me know what kind of series you're thinking about. If possible, also include a specific example so I can read the books!

13

WRITER, KNOW THYSELF

In order to be successful at writing a series, you need to know yourself. You need to know what kind of a writer you are, what motivates you, and how and when you do your best work.

First, let's talk about why you're writing. If your definition of success is based around spending time every day as a writer, then your experience and schedule is going to be very different from someone whose goal is around income generation and volume of books.

If you know what kind of a writer you are and WHY you are writing, that allows you to know best how to motivate yourself and how to structure your days, weeks, months and years. The thing about writing a series is that the scope and scale is flexible. If it's going well and you love it, then you could (in theory) write in one series for decades, or even your entire writing life! Diana Gabaldon's *Outlander* series is a great example of this.

What do you need to know about yourself before you dive in?

There's an awful lot of psychology involved in being a writer. And when it comes to being a series author, that is even more true than usual. Because if you're writing stand-alone books, you can up and change projects, story worlds, characters or whatever you want if you hit a block or if you get tired of the genre you're writing in. You can detour any time you want.

One of the challenges that is unique to writing a series is that you will have some aspects of your stories that stay the same from book to book, maybe even throughout the entire series.

Will you be not just okay with that, but be able to stay passionate about what you're doing?

You need to know your own limits. If you're the kind of person who is easily distracted or your creativity feeds off of variety, or you love diving into new things but aren't so good at maintaining the existing stuff, then you need to make sure the way you structure your series doesn't tie you into the same thing, book after book, because you'll become frustrated and bored, and that will make it difficult (if not impossible) for you to be producing your best work. And if you lose momentum and interest, so will your readers.

If you find it difficult to generate new characters and you don't love that part of the book-writing process, then you might think about writing a series that features the same main characters in each book.

If you love to travel and combine that with your writing, then you might want to ensure your character (s) have the ability or requirement to travel, so that your potential locations are many and varied.

If you like to write different kinds of stories and you don't like being too penned in, then think about writing a limited series, like a trilogy and see how you feel once that's done.

Your Turn

- What are your favourite parts of the writing process?
- What are your least favourite parts of the writing process?
- How long can you envision yourself working on the "same" project before you get bored and either drop it or move on to something else?

14

DEFINE YOUR SERIES

Why does the type of series matter?

When considering all the tools and systems you could choose to use to track the details associated with your stories, the *kind* of series you're writing influences which tools will be most helpful to set you up for success writing future books.

For example: If you're writing several stories that all take place on the same fictional planet, but none of the characters or events overlap, you will want to focus on tracking the world-building elements.

If you're writing a series that features the same group of characters, in the same locations, and all the stories are happening simultaneously then you'll need to track information about the timeline, the events happening, and all the characters as well as the location details to make sure you are consistent from book to book.

If you're writing a series where your main character is the only consistent element from story to story, and all the stories occur in a linear timeline then you'll need to focus your planning and tracking systems on your character's history and recording the details of what has happened to them in each story (e.g. injuries, new memories, new friends, new enemies made, etc.)

As you can imagine, these options vary in complexity and the amount of information and detail-tracking required. As you're deciding what kind of series to write, think about what will suit your personality and writing style—not just in terms of story-telling but story management, too.

Your Turn

- What kind of a series are you currently writing?
- What is the element that ties your stories together?
- Is there more than one element? (For example, a group of people, an event *and* a setting.)
- What excites you most during your writing process? (For instance, world-building, developing new characters, digging into unexpected action sequences, researching new locations through travel.)
- Are there any aspects of the storytelling or story-tracking that you tend to avoid, gloss over or view as work more than fun?
- Look at the two lists you just made. Are there any

types of connections in series that you might want
to cross off your list of potentials?

- Do you have a sense of how long your attention
  span is or how long you think you might stay
  happy and engaged on one series?

15
—————

MAP YOUR CONNECTIONS

What does mapping connections refer to?

If you've chosen any kind of series other than where the only connection is the main character, or it's really one story broken into parts—then you'll need to know how the books and stories relate to each other and how you will lead your readers through your story world. How you will entice them to make the leap with you from one book to the next.

That's what I mean by map your connections. Even if you do only have one main character, having the order of your stories laid out in front of you before you get started, can be very helpful for ensuring your readers *have* to read the next story in the series.

I call it mapping because while you can just write down how things are connected, it can also be useful to have this information in a visual format.

Here are a couple of examples of connection maps for my *Rivers End Romance* stories. I sometimes use temporary covers, or even just coloured squares with names if I know them. Then I swap them out for the real covers as they're ready.

Map for the MacAllisters of Rivers End

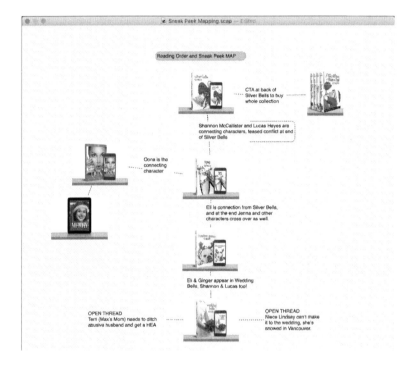

Map for multiple mini-series within larger world

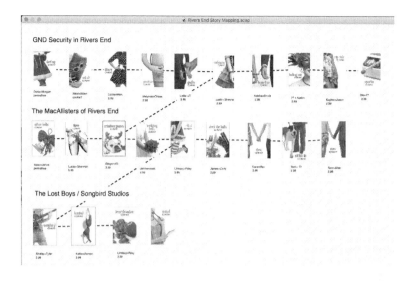

Why would you want to map connections?

This is useful in a few different ways, and likely in some ways you won't even realize until you've written a few books in your series.

1. Gain clarity about your type of series

Mapping connections will force you to be clear about what elements connect your stories together. This will help you decide what to track and how best to track that information. This will give you a head start on the sections that follow.

2. Determine reading order

It may seem obvious if you're writing your first series that you start at book one and work your way through the stories. But what if you have a series with multiple entry points, such as a series where each book is connected by characters, not a timeline?

What if you have several distinct stories that are all written in the same world but are connected by a single story thread, the way many science fiction and fantasy stories are?

Or, you have a character from one series who is the connector to the next set of stories, the way Nora Roberts connect her series' stories?

You need to guide your readers confidently from one story to the next in the way that gives them the optimal reading experience. That is what will keep them coming back for more of your books.

3. Track open story threads

It's important to give your readers the satisfaction they're looking for. Too many open story threads, either in one story or across a series, can leave readers feeling unsatisfied. It's one thing to purposely lead them along an arc that spans a whole trilogy or longer, but you don't want to leave anyone hanging. And ideally, you'll wrap up some open threads right in the next book... which will help people keep reading along in your series. For example, you could see two open threads leading away from *Wedding Bells* in the *MacAllisters of Rivers End* series map.

Open thread #1: Terri needs a HEA (Happily Ever After), far away from her abusive husband. While I didn't intend to originally give her a story, readers related so strongly to her, and asked about when she would get her HEA that I decided to add a story into the series for her.

Open thread #2: Niece Lindsay doesn't make it to Jenna and Isaac's wedding at the end of *Wedding Bells*. She's the lead in character to a new trilogy... so when we close her story loop in the *MacAllisters* series, we will open a whole new series of loops and characters into *The Lost Boys/Songbird Studios* mini-series. You can see that crossover point mapped on the larger story map.

How will you map the connections between stories?

There are lots of different tools to help you keep track of or map these connections.

1. Pen/pencil and paper

You don't need fancy software. You need clarity and understanding. You can use a piece of paper and a pen to mind map your ideas using simple boxes with titles and arrows to get your mind—and series connections—clear.

2. Scapple or other mind mapping software

I'm a fan of Scapple for mind mapping as it's made by the same folks who created Scrivener, which is what I use to write the books in my series. Scapple is quick and easy to use, as well as a very reasonable one-time payment of $24 at the time of writing this book. That's what the sample maps were made with.

3. Website timeline plugin

If you want a creative and visual way to guide readers through your stories in a particular order, there are several website plugins and tools available to help. I have a simple event timeline on my website (https://cjhuntromance. com/timeline/) that acts to map the connections between my stories from date perspective. It's a subtle way to let my readers know which stories in the series they might need to "catch up on."

PRO TIP: Your reader journey map will also come in handy when you're setting prices, running promotions and discounts, and deciding which books to run your paid ads on. We'll cover this in more detail in the section on scaling up your sales.

Your Turn

- Review the options for mapping your stories in your series. How will you apply this information? What mind mapping tool will you try first?
- Map out the planned books in your series using titles or book covers.
- Include directional arrows if your overall story and linkages are linear or if you want readers to work their way through the stories in a specific order.

16

PLAN YOUR ARC

If you're writing a series or mini-series that has a linear timeline or an overarching story thread, it's smart to have a roughed-out plot arc for the whole series or mini-series storyline before you start writing.

Having a plot arc will help you ensure you've got enough meaty stuff to keep your characters interesting throughout the series, help you see the best place to end one story and start the next, and give you information to drop hints in just the right places to keep the reader following that reader journey you mapped earlier.

Your Turn

- Is your series arc based on a character or your world or something else?
- If it's tied together by character, how does that character develop from story to story?
- If it's based on events in a world, how do those escalate from book to book?
- What are the key turning points in your series arc?

PRO TIP: If you're not sure how to energetically map out your series arc, you might find *The Plot Whisperer* by Martha Alderson to be a useful book.

How many books should you break your overall story arc into?

Part of planning your series arc is deciding how you want to break up your story into separate chunks (books, novellas, short stories—or some combination). What factors go into making this decision?

- What length of books you're comfortable writing.
- Genre expectations around length.
- Where the good "mini-arcs" are in your story (aka where does it make sense to stop and start the story?).
- Your attention span (will you get bored by book 3? Or 9?).
- Are cliffhangers acceptable in your genre?
- Traditional or indie? (If you're thinking traditional,

publishers *generally* won't commit to long series—
they want to see if it sells first and then commit to
a book or two at a time).

- Your marketing/business plan.

First, we'll tackle a common question I've come across at
this stage.

Can't I just write a trilogy and then make it longer if I want at the end?

Well, yeah. People have done that. And certain types of
series are way more fitting for that approach than others.
Let's look at a couple examples.

Case Study #1:

Trent has an idea for a series based around a CIA agent
who is constantly traveling around the world having
adventures. The only character who shows up in all the
books is the CIA protagonist. The location, the people, the
problem—those are all different from book to book.
Because there's no specific story arc that operates through
all of the books, Trent isn't tied to a certain number of
books. If he gets tired of writing them, he can stop. He
won't be tied into writing X more books to ensure a
satisfying ending to the story to avoid creating a horde of
angry fans.

Case Study #2:

Bonnie has an awesome dragon book that's really, really
long. It's come in at 200,000 words and she knows that's
way too long for one book. Since series sell and she knows

that, her plan is to break the book into three parts and publish it as a trilogy, releasing all three books in really quick succession.

This can absolutely work.

But what about book four?

If sales show Bonnie that readers love her dragon story world and characters, she'd do well to look at the overall story arc and her options for ways to extend the series that won't result in something that feels "tacked on" or like an afterthought—even though it very well may be.

For example, instead of effectively adding another act in the existing story series, Bonnie could write another trilogy that features one of the other characters from the original series as the new hero. Or, she could age her world and write a series featuring the next generation of characters, so that her original books become the history of the world.

Case Study #3:

I'm going to use myself. I started my series knowing that I'd be writing several mini-series based on families, with overlapping characters. But I didn't have a clear arc for how all the different family's mini-series fit together. I wrote "Book One" for several of the family's series' stories. The challenge this presented was that readers were then waiting for the next book in ALL of the different mini-series.

Starting my series this way was what I needed to do to figure out how all the stories fit together and to get the key timeline set. Creatively, it totally made sense to do it that way. *But*, as I learned from my sales data, that wasn't a strategic series author way to write from a business point of view. When I finished one mini-series arc, the MacAllister's story, it became clear that readers wanted to read through one family's story, not jump from family to family, despite the connections between the stories.

PRO TIP: If at all possible commit to one story arc or mini-series at a time. Something that gives you a "finished" product to be marketing while you're working on your next set of books.

What about ending the book with a cliffhanger?

Be careful about ending a book on a cliffhanger. Yes, it *can* be a great way to get readers to pick up your next book. But, it can also make them angry and frustrated. Know your genre conventions and reader expectations on this point. How do you know what is okay and what isn't? Read the reviews on other people's books. The good ones, and the bad ones. Readers will tell you what they didn't like. And be sure to mention it up front at the end of your book description so readers can opt out if necessary. While this seems counterintuitive, if you have a sale where you end up with an unhappy reader and a bad review—it might have been better not to have that sale at all!

For example, if you have a romance series, you can potentially get away with having a cliffhanger ending for a subplot to lead people into the next book. However, you don't usually want to leave your couple in an unresolved situation. At the very least they need a Happily For Now

(HFN), and ideally their Happily Ever After (HEA) will soon follow.

If you *are* going to leave folks hanging, make sure that next book is coming really soon!

How does writing speed impact your decisions about how to break up your series?

How fast can you complete the books? If you're a fantasy author who can reliably commit to writing 500 words a day and you are planning an epic series of seven books that are 120,000 words long, you'll be committing to approximately five years of writing in that same series (and that assumes every word you write it good and you're not doing extensive rewrites).

Are you comfortable with that? Or does it put a lead-like sick feeling in the pit of your stomach?

Will you feel excited and focused with that as your goal or totally trapped and panicky?

You need to consider your overall commitment to the project, the time available to complete it, how that fits into your plans for the development of your writing career and more.

How much context or backstory from previous books should you include in the ones that follow?

This is tricky. I know I get really irritated when people repeat too much information from previous books. You will want to include enough that people are able to understand what they are reading, but not so much that if they read your whole series in a row it'll feel repetitive. Leaving things a little open and hinting at what happened in other books can be a great way to encourage read-through on your series! Some tips of how to carry this off well:

- Avoid what we call an "info dump" where you include a whole bunch of information from a previous book all at once.
- Weave backstory in naturally, and only when it's directly relevant and important to help the reader understand the meaning or significance of the current scene.
- Leave some things for people to discover in the other books. As long as they can understand the current story, it's okay for them to get the more in-depth meaning when they go back and read earlier books.
- Assume your readers are smart (because they are!).

Some things to consider and a case study

Before you decide how to tackle this in your own series, let's run through the logic I used when making this choice for myself.

I originally intended to write all standalone, full-length romance novels in the *Rivers End Romance* series. But when I looked at all the angles, this is what I was dealing with:

- What is effective at building a readership in romance? *Series sell better and readers love them.*

- What works best to generate sales momentum? *Frequent releases.*
- What lengths am I comfortable and experienced at writing? *10-30K words is a length I know I can complete.*
- How long would it take me to make all the stories I had outlined into full length novels? *Like, 150+ years.*
- How many products/books do most authors need before readers and other authors consider them an established author? *In romance, 5-10 books seems to be the tipping point.*
- How many products do authors need to start generating a decent, liveable income from their fiction? *I used the benchmark from the 20BooksTo50K facebook group as a guideline—the idea that you need 20 decently selling books to reach 50 thousand dollars a year in income.*
- What conditions do I need to perfect my writing and publishing process? *Lots of completed projects with a regular release schedule in a compressed period to test and evolve my processes.*
- How could I get entry into alternate markets? *Shorter stories were an affordable way to learn how audiobook production works.*
- How could I keep costs affordable on the publishing side? *Shorter works were more affordable for editing, and quicker to make available, and I could take revenue from released products and re-direct it to new ones.*
- What kind/length of stories do I love to read?

Christmas romance novellas, romance with magical elements, romantic comedy, and romantic suspense.

- When could I schedule breaks in my client consulting work to focus on writing? *Over summer, and Christmas break primarily.*
- How long would my attention span last? *I love learning new things, changing gears often and hate feeling trapped in anything… so within my series I needed room to follow the energy and the passion into different groups of stories, different themes, and different sub-genres.*

What did this tell me? That my most effective strategy would be to write a linked mini-series of holiday romance novellas, that I could write over the summer and then be ready to release during the fall season. I'd be able to focus on promotion over the Christmas season, and have audiobooks produced in my busier work season (spring) since most of the work is done by other folks on those. Those could come out in advance of calmer summer season, and be ready for the following holiday season. Then, if I liked what I saw when I evaluated my sales data, I could just repeat it all again with another mini-series and another round of new releases—changing anything I thought could be better about my processes along the way.

Your Turn

Make a list (like the one I did above) of all the things that will be key drivers or limitations in this decision for you. Think about:

- Your business goals

- Your personality
- The expectations of your genre's readers
- What length of story you love to read
- What length of story you love to write
- The amount of time you have to dedicate to your writing career
- Length and scope of commitment you're comfortable making to this series
- Financial commitment you're comfortable making to this series before you see returns on your investment
- Anything else you think will impact the writing of your series and your ability to commit to the project

Look at your list and see what it tells you. Where is your best chance for success? Where are the opportunities that are uniquely suited to you and your situation?

17

BUILD YOUR WORLD

World-building is a huge topic, and depending on your genre you will need to do varying amounts of this.

If you're writing contemporary romance series set in your own real-life city, for example, most of your world-building will already be done for you.

If you're writing a fantasy series in a completely original world, you're going to spend a lot more time in this world-building phase.

You are going to need a system to track any rules that you've developed for your world so that you're consistent throughout. This might include things like:

- The language your characters speak, and specific words in that language
- The history of your world

- Weather and seasons
- Calendar and how time is tracked
- Cultural information about different groups who live there
- How family structure works
- What kinds of clothing people wear
- Naming conventions
- Modes of transportation
- And much, much more

How to track your world-building details

There are many options for how to do this. Some people use a journal or notebook, or collage reference images like a scrapbook.

But if you're looking at a series, especially one that may run for many books (and years of your life), you might prefer to have something digital that is searchable, portable, and can grow with you as your world expands with each additional title.

If you are co-creating the world with collaborators, make sure your tools and systems will work for all parties and exist in a format in which everyone can access the most current versions of the world-building files.

1. Google Docs (free)

Google Docs is a great tool for collaborative writing. It has many of the same functions and features as Microsoft Word. It allows you to easily bookmark different sections in your document, is searchable and can handle multiple users doing updates.

2. Google Sheets (free)/ Excel ($) / Numbers ($)

If you're tracking information that makes more sense in columns and/or different tabbed sheets and you want it to be easily searchable, one of these spreadsheet options would be a great tool for you.

3. Scrivener ($)

Scrivener is a tool designed specifically for writers. It includes the option to create folders for your research and world-building elements. It's trickier to share files if you're collaborating with other writers unless you keep the file in shared Dropbox, for instance.

What if you're writing in a shared world that is not yours?

If you are writing in a shared world that is not your own creation, then you will likely be provided with an information packet of some kind—effectively a world bible —when you are invited to the project. This might come up in situations where you're co-authoring a book with someone in their established world, or if you've been hired by a publisher or book packager to write one (or more) of a series of books where there will be multiple authors contributing.

In either of these cases, you will likely be given what information already exists, along with instructions on how to add to it if that is something you are allowed to do. If you are writing in a shared world—if this information is not provided, you should request it. You must be clear on the parameters before you dive into the project. If they are expecting you to read the entire series and figure out the recurring details yourself, you will need to budget that into your timelines, and make sure you're okay with the additional work that creates for you!

Your Turn: for new series authors

- What kind of world-building details are going to be relevant for your stories?
- Brainstorm a list. (Refer to the list that follows the Your Turn section for ideas.)

Your Turn: for established series authors

- Think about your last book(s). What details in your world did you use from previous books that you might need to refer to in future ones?
- Do you have a current system you're happy with for tracking these details?
- Is there anything about your current world-building tracking system that you would like to improve?

Some world-building details you might need to track

- Where is this world located?
- What is the geography like? Flat? Mountainous? Covered in water?
- What is the climate like? Warm? Cold?
- How does this impact the type of creatures that live there?
- Are there towns or cities here?
- What kind of cycle do the days have here? Is there night and day?
- Where does light come from? Heat?
- Is there gravity?
- What are the natural resources of this place?
- Why would people want to live here? Why wouldn't they?
- Who or what lives in this place?
- Do they live in family groups? Alone? In peer groups?
- How do they survive?
- What kind of society are they? Peaceful? Technological?
- What senses do they have?
- How do they get around in their world?
- What kind of houses or structures do they have?
- What kind of clothing or protective body parts (like an extra arm for fighting off bandits, or bulletproof skin) do your characters have?
- How do they communicate with each other?
- Do they eat? If so, what? If not, how do they get their energy?

NOTE: I recommend you *not* choose a tool until you've worked through the next three sections. Ideally, you'll find systems and tools that will work for all areas of your tracking.

18

TRACK YOUR TIMELINE

Another aspect of your story that needs to be tracked is the timeline of events that take place in your world. Sometimes you'll only need to track the events that actually happen in your story, but more likely, you'll also want some way to make note of what happened in the past because it's part of the shared experiences different characters in the same world will have.

For example, if you have several books that all occur during the same Christmas holiday, and it snows on Christmas Eve in one story, you'd better not have characters out carolling under a bright full moon in one of the other stories!

Linear timeline

In some cases, all you will need to create to keep your series events in order is a simple linear timeline. For example, if your story arc is that two neighbours had a big feud over who made the best eggnog in 1996 (Book 1), then didn't speak for ten years (Book 2), and then reconciled in 2006 at which point their children met (Book 3) and then later got married (Book 4), a linear timeline should be enough to stay organized in your series.

However, if you write the story arc above as separate stories of all the siblings who grew up with that feud as a defining factor in their lives, you'll need to keep track of potentially dozens of specific events that happened during that ten-year period, with events potentially weaving through all the stories. In this situation you will need to create simultaneous timelines.

Simultaneous timelines

Tracking events in multiple books with simultaneous timelines is a bit trickier. Personally, I have had the most luck with using a program called Aeon Timeline. It allows me to visually see possible intersection points in my story lines. That said, I always start old school, by marking up a giant whiteboard when I'm in the brainstorming phase, because I don't enter anything into my master **series timeline** until it's "written in stone." More on that in the next section with tips specific to Aeon Timeline.

Regardless of how you're creating your working timeline it's smart to have a "finished for real" timeline that you keep handy and up to date as you learn new things about events in your story. You never know when one of those events will make an appearance in a future story. And, having that list of events can also be used to inspire story elements in future books if you find yourself stuck on a plot point.

What does your tool or system need to do?

Ideally the tool or system you use needs to let you see at a glance where each person was in relation to a specific event on that timeline so you can answer these questions:

- Where were they when that happened?
- Were they involved directly?
- Would they have heard the details of what happened?
- How old were they when it happened?
- What else was going on in their life that would have impacted how they reacted to those events?
- Who would they have gone to in order to work through the events?
- What kind of an impact would it have had on them?

Invented calendar/time system

But what if you invented your system of time? Perhaps you're writing a sci-fi fantasy story with both a 236 day year and time travel. For now, just make a note of all the things you'll need to track and then pay particular attention to the Aeon Timeline tool mentioned below.

Tools to track your stories' timeline(s)

1. Use your wall

If the events in your series are fairly straightforward, chart paper or sticky notes on your wall may be all you need. I know of writers who've turned entire walls into a chalkboard or a whiteboard using special paint so they can write directly on their walls. I have whiteboard walls myself. Best thing I ever did!

2. Word Document

One step up from paper and pen versions is using a Word doc to keep track of your timeline. This makes it portable which is imperative if you write in spaces not inside your papered-up or markable walls.

3. Scrivener

If you use Scrivener for writing, you may find keeping your timeline in this software is the most convenient place for it. Making a timeline in Scrivener works nicely when you have really clear events that occur in a linear fashion. You can just create a timeline document in your research folder, and add each event as it occurs. The benefit of Scrivener is that you can easily include as much detail about each major event as you like. If you're including lots of details about each event, you want want to create a whole timeline folder and make each event a scene inside that folder.

4. One Stop for Writers

One Stop for Writers (https://onestopforwriters.com/) has a wealth of very cool tools all in one place that will help you with time lining events (as well as just about every other area of writing). It's the brain child of the authors of the *Writers' Thesaurus* series Angela Ackerman and Becca Puglisi, who partnered up with Lee Powell, the creator of Scrivener for Windows and and Scapple for Windows.

5. Aeon Timeline

As I mentioned, Aeon timeline is my favourite tool for keeping track of events. It takes a few hours to get the hang of it, but if you follow the tutorials and set things up properly it can save you many hours in the long haul. It also has the benefit of being scalable as you can just keep adding things to it, and it's also able to handle multiple types of information.

Aeon Timeline allows you to associate events with people, locations, projects, story arcs, and more–collectively known within Aeon Timeline as **entities.** Entities have a name and a type (e.g. Person, Location) as defined in the chosen template, and can have relationships with any number of events.

Entities can also have start/birth and end/death dates or events, from which Aeon Timeline can calculate ages.

In truth, pretty much everything you'll ever need to track can be handled by Aeon Timeline. And it integrates with Scrivener which is fantastic.

A couple of things to note when you're using it for a **series.** You may want to have separate timelines for your individual books and your series/world as a whole.

For example, I will often use a separate timeline file for each book as I'm planning and plotting if it's complex enough to need that (and you can sync that with Scrivener), and then just manually add any key events to my **series** timeline document as a reference if any of my events cross over with things that have happened in the other books, or other mini-series. I generally do this after I've finished writing and editing the current WIP—I go back into the main series timeline and jot down events once they're "written in stone." That's part of my cleanup process for each book, and helps immensely when it comes to see how existing events fit with plotting and planning the next book.

Your Turn

- What do you need to track on your timeline?
- Investigate the tool options, and see which ones feel like a good fit for your series, your personality and your writing process.
- Test them out, one by one (most paid tools have a free trial period).
- Brainstorm as many possible "exceptions to the rule" you can think of. What would break each system you test? How well will each system work if your series were to grow to five or ten or more titles?
- Identify a couple of "best possibilities."

NOTE: I recommend you *not* choose a tool until you've worked through the next two sections. Ideally, you'll find systems and tools that will work for all areas of your tracking.

19

TRACK YOUR PLACES

Tracking the individual places in your stories is important to help your story consistency—both within a book and between books.

If you do this consistently and strategically it's going to have a myriad of benefits for you.

It's going to **save you time** because once you've created a location in detail you can easily revisit your notes on that place without having to re-create it in your mind.

It's going to **eliminate hassle** because it will ensure your accuracy which means you won't have your superfans sending you messages about not having gotten the details right. (And they will. Seriously.)

It's going to **save you money before you publish** because your editor will not need to spend time finding and fixing continuity issues. You'll be able to simply point them in the direction of your **places** document if they need to verify something.

It's going to **save you money after you publish** (if you're indie) because if you get all the details right the first time you won't have to pay for revisions after your readers point out mistakes to you.

If your goal is to **pitch** your series, your knowledge of your locations will come through in your writing and will help you come across as organized, professional and with a keen eye for detail. All good things when an agent or editor is trying to decide if they want to enter into an ongoing working relationship with someone.

Okay, so now you get *why* you should be tracking the places in your series. But *how* the heck do you manage that?

Whether you're using places that actually exist or fictional places you've created, there are a whole whack of things you'll need to know and keep track of. These things might include:

- Floor plans for businesses and houses
- Layout of a town
- Type of furnishings or decor
- The ambience of a place
- The people associated with that place
- The history of a house or business

In many ways, your places are just like your characters.

But I can imagine that right now your heart is racing a little and you're having a bit of a mental meltdown. Because, *Holy crap, my characters visit about a million places and I'll never be able to track all those things for all those places and…*

Okay. Take a breath.

Exactly the same way that you have main characters that get the full-meal deal when it comes to planning and detail tracking, and then supporting cast members who you don't get to know quite as well until they take on a more integral role in the story, you can also have primary locations and supporting locations.

Let's dive into a real-life example for a minute.

Some series have key locations that characters come back to book after book (whether it's the same characters or different ones). In the *Rivers End* series, I have people in various stories visit the local pub, Just One More. Because it features heavily in many of the stories, I took the time to actually create detailed floor plans of that pub so that I knew roughly the size, the capacity, the layout, where the band would play, if there were differences between how it was set up on the weekend versus a quiet weekday afternoon. I made up a roster of the staff and what nights they worked. And, I know some of the history of the place and its owner—at least enough that I can drop interesting —and consistent—hints and tidbits in the stories.

For the places my characters haven't yet visited and ones that likely will never be feature locations, I just list the name of the location and a single word or short phrase to track what I have said about it. Then if my characters do end up spending more time there later and my "walk on" location gets upgraded to a "feature role" in the future, I'll have a record of what I've said about it so I don't contradict myself.

Tools to track your stories' places

1. Word or Google Docs file (Free)

If you're not dealing with a ton of locations, a Word doc may be all you need. If you've got a lot of places, or if you're collaborating with someone you'd like to be able to see/edit the list of places, then a Google Docs file could work better. If you've got a lot of places you might want to bookmark sections to make yourself a functioning table of contents so it's easy to jump around in your document and find what you're looking for. You may find it helpful to break your document into world-building stuff, and then track your world, your places (towns, etc.) and your specific locations (Jenny's house, the pub, etc.).

2. Spreadsheet or Google Sheet (Free)

Personally, I usually prefer a spreadsheet over a Word document as it's easier to add more columns and rows to your template as things develop in your series and your process. You can drag in floor plans, site descriptions, list which books the locations appear in—whatever will be most useful to you. And I find Google Sheets easy to link to from other documents (you'll see why that matters later).

3. Scrivener ($)

Scrivener comes with a preloaded folder to track your locations. You can create separate "chapters" for each of your main locations to keep all the information about that place in one easy-to-reference spot. If you have certain places that turn up throughout your series, you can even save that locational info as part of the template you load for each new project.

4. Aeon Timeline ($)

As I mentioned in **Chapter 18: Track your timeline**, Aeon Timeline can track way more than just timelines. And one of the things it's set up to do is track locations.

Your Turn: for new series authors

- Make a list of the places you know your characters will visit.
- Brainstorm the kinds of details you need to keep track of about the places in your series.
- Evaluate the options you identified in the timeline section and see if they will work to track your places as well. If not, what other tool would you need to integrate to track your places? How would those two work together?
- Remember to wind time forward three to five years… imagine you have several more books in your series. Will the system you're considering still work then? Can it grow with your needs?

Your Turn: for established series authors

- If you haven't already done so, make a list of all of the places that are featured in your books.
- List the specific details that you've mentioned about each location.
- Evaluate the options you identified in the timeline section and see if they will work to track your places as well. If not, what other tool would you need to integrate to track your places? How would those two work together?
- Remember to wind time forward three to five years... imagine you have several more books in your series. Will the system you're considering still work then? Can it grow with your needs?

NOTE: Nope, you're still not making a final choice. We've got to figure out how tracking your characters is going to work in this set of tools first!

20

TRACK YOUR CHARACTERS

When you create a series, you need to keep track of all your characters so they are consistent from book to book. Nothing screams amateur (and sucks people out of your story) like having a recurring character whose personality or appearance changes without reason from one story to another. All the little details matter.

And let me tell you (she says with the experience of someone who did *not* get this advice early enough) it is much easier to do this *as you go*. Knowing that time is one of your precious resources, I can assure you that there are much better things to spend yours on than having to extract all those details from all your books *after* you've got a few of them done!

Also, if you're producing multiple formats of your book (like print and audiobooks in addition to your eBooks) or even just paying someone to format your eBooks for you, it can be quite expensive to make changes to those other formats.

What kinds of things do you need to know about your characters and why?

1. Physical descriptions

It's extremely important to be consistent with the physical descriptions of your characters, as that's what your readers are using to form their pictures of the people who move around in your story world. If you suddenly change a detail, it highlights the fact that this individual is make-believe. Readers hate that.

I have a hard time remembering these descriptions—especially when one of my characters changes appearance over time. For me, the best way to keep track of what people look like is to find a photo—or series of photos—to represent each of my characters.

There are dozens of free stock image sites that allow you to download and use images for non-commercial purposes. You can pin these images to a Pinterest board, save them in your Word document or in Scrivener, or add them to your website as a feature for readers. Any time you can make your research double as a bonus feature you're doing your future self a favour! You might then use these photos to help make a visual map of each character's relationships by creating some kind of family tree.

I've shared photos of all the residents of Rivers End with my readers on my website—which is also a quick and easy place for me to find them when I need a refresher about a character's eye colour or what their hair looks like. (https://cjhuntromance.com/explore-rivers-end/people/)

One caution, though: not all readers want to see your ideas about what your characters look like in the form of an actual photo. Some people want to create that picture in their heads. This doesn't mean you shouldn't share that information—it just means you should be respectful about how you present it. Make sure any webpage with character photos is clearly identified as such and, if you share photos in your newsletter, give readers a heads-up to stop reading if they don't want to see your idea characters' appearances.

You may also want to track things about the way your characters move, and if they have any distinguishing physical characteristics or habits. For example, do they walk with a limp when the weather is bad because of an old injury in their knee?

2. Speech and dialogue patterns

You want to make sure that all your characters don't sound the same. Particularly for newer writers, you may find that all your characters at first sound like you! But each person in your story world needs their own voice.

A good way to distinguish between characters is to give them consistent elements of speech that are unique to them. You could have a character who is trying to quit swearing and makes up creative alternatives to curse words, a character who speaks in very short sentences and always gets right to the point, someone with a stutter, or someone with an accent (although do your homework here, since writing in accents is challenging!).

When you're dealing with a lot of characters, it will really help you to have a tracking list. It will help you in the writing, and revision process, and it will also help your editor to have a guide to refer back to when editing your story.

3. Personality traits

You need to keep track of who your characters are at their core. If you have someone who is a total bully in book one and then is nice to everyone in book three, you better make sure there's a reason for that personality change or your readers will lose faith in you as a reliable story guide. If you've worked through Eileen Cook's, *Build Better Characters*— a book on using psychological tools to develop your character's backstory—you could track the key details of what you learned about your characters in your character sketches folder.

4. Emotional wound and overall character arc

It's important to know each of your main character's emotional wounds because that wound will impact every decision they make in your books. Even if it's a minor character, the authenticity will be much greater if the reader sees them behave consistently throughout your series.

Having consistent personality traits also gives you a solid baseline to work from when it's time for your character to change and grow. In most series, your main characters—at least—should have some kind of arc where they learn something, change in some way or grow up emotionally.

Save the Cat! Writes a Novel by Jessica Brody does an excellent job of explaining a character's arc, goal, problem and the need to flesh out a believable character by answering a set of very useful questions if you want to deep dive into this area.

Knowing your main characters' emotional wounds is especially important if you have a series that follows a single character over multiple books, whether they grow or not. Consider Sherlock Holmes, for example. As a character he does not grow from story to story, but he does have very consistent character traits which can be linked back to his emotional wound.

If you're not sure what I'm talking about when I say emotional wound, check out *The Emotional Wound Thesaurus* by Angela Ackerman and Becca Puglisi for some extra credit reading. It's fantastic. I highly recommend the print version of this book. I write my characters' names on sticky notes and put them into the book where their emotional wound is described. This not only allows me easy quick and access to character traits I can expect my characters to exhibit, I often troll through the index of wounds and flip to pages without stickies when I'm in the character creation phase, so not to create too many people with the same wound.

5. History

In order to know why a character has a certain wound or motivation, we need to understand what has happened to them in their past. This means we, as writers, need to know enough about their history to ensure they are reacting to events in a realistic way. We also need to know which events in our story's timeline each of our characters might have been present for—in the past, present or future if you're doing time travel!

You don't need to know every little detail but knowing the basics for each character will really help with that authenticity piece, and will make your job as the writer easier.

6. Relationships

People, including characters in our books, tend to define ourselves largely by our relationships with others, so you need to track those relationships. This includes spouse(s), children, parents, grandparents, best friend now and in grade school, pets... You need to know how your characters fit into their world, and you need to document that so that the details are consistent from book to book.

If your character makes some small throwaway comment about their brother in book two and then in book four they have only three sisters—you'll have some 'splainin' to do to your astute readers who will point this error out to you.

7. Dates of milestones

I can see how you wouldn't think it's important to always know a character's birthday. I mean, sure if it's the character's birthday as a central part of the story then yes, you'll need to mention it. But for most people, that won't be relevant. Is it still worth keeping track of for every character?

The short answer, *Yes, it totally is.*

Many of the details about who we are have been determined by when we were born. The popularity of certain names, the world events we will have witnessed or that will have impacted the world we live in, where we are in birth order, how close a birthday is to another major holiday, the cohort of other folks we went to school with, the likelihood of us knowing a certain song or what kind of car we might have driven in high school... all are dependent partly on when we were born. Knowing the birth date and birth location of your character gives you a major head start in knowing who they are and what they're all about.

What is the best way to keep track of all this?

Now we come to the million-dollar question... well, two questions really.

- How are we supposed to keep track of all this?
- How much of this do we need to know before we get started writing?

The good news is you don't need to answer all these details about every character before you start writing. In fact, I'd actually recommend you don't pin down your secondary characters too completely before you get started, as you never know what roles you might need them to look after in the story.

However, in the case of your main characters in each story —or in the ensemble cast if you have a group of characters tying your series together—you should know a great deal about their wounds, their arcs, and their roles before you get started. There's always room to discover new and interesting bits of their history, but you want to make sure the basic elements are solid before you embark on writing a whole book—or series of books—around them.

For supporting characters, and for details that are not pivotal to the entire plot, you can literally make it up as you go. The most important take-away is to remember to document important new character details as you add them.

Does that mean noting those details on your master tracking sheet the second you write them down in your draft? Not at all. But a quick scan through your pages at the end of each writing day is a good way to handle it. That way your records will always be 100 percent up-to-date which means when you sit down for your next writing sprint and you need to quickly reference a detail, you're not scrolling through pages of writing, tempting yourself to *just briefly* slip into editing mode. Oh no. Thou shalt not break the flow of the writing for the sake of "organization."

Document them where? What is this mysterious tracking place of which you speak?

You're going to document details in your handy dandy tracking system. I'm being purposely vague here because if you're following my directions, you haven't decided on your tool(s) yet… or at least not fully.

Your Turn

- Take out your journal or open your document on your device and brainstorm all the specific aspects of your characters you will need to document.
- Are you already using some kind of system to track your characters?
- *If yes:* Does it keep track of all the things you brainstormed? Does it play nice with any other tools you may be using to track world-building details, timeline and places?
- *If yes,* great! *If no,* we need to work on that. Identify all the things that are missing from your current system, or that aren't working as well as you think they should be.
- Think about what tools you identified in the previous two sections as being good possibilities. Will they work to track your characters as well?
- If yes, great. You might be ready to commit!
- If no, think about how you could add an additional element to your system to make it work.
- If you've figured out the perfect solution for yourself, then it's time to commit. If you're not sure how the pieces could go together, take a look at the example below then circle back to this question.

And no, **you don't have to pick just one tool.** Sometimes what works best is a combination. I have used ALL of these tools at different times and in different ways as things evolved in my stories and my process. What you see described below is my current system, along with explanations of why I chose to do things a certain way.

Google Sheets

I use Google Sheets for my Rivers End town business directory, and character database. I drag in pictures of the people to the spreadsheet along with key info about them. Why Google Sheets? It's shareable so it's easy for Amanda, my editor, to reference what people look like while she's doing her work on my stories.

Dropbox folder

I keep my digitized town maps, scanned sketches of floor plans for locations that recur throughout the series, and all the source files of my character images in one Dropbox folder so they're easy to find and reference.

Aeon Timeline

I use Aeon Timeline for my high-level timeline of events that could impact more than one book in the series. Although it's possible, I do not sync this timeline with Scrivener. I update it manually after each book is finished and use it during planning for future books. But I also include a single-book timeline "underneath" the main one so the entire series is in one document. That makes it really easy to see how everything fits together.

Scrivener

I have one Scrivener file for each mini-series that is home for all the stories in that series. In each Scrivener file I have a "planning" section that contains all the info specific to that mini-series. This way, it's super easy to find and refer to what happened in other books, make notes when something changes in the current manuscript that's going to impact other stories, and can include links wherever they're most relevant to Google Sheets and Dropbox files that are helpful.

———

Your Turn

- Review the tools that you think will work best for the information you need to track.
- Download trial versions of paid services and put them to the test with details about your world, timelines, places and character details.
- If you've already written a few books in your series, published or not, once you're happy with your tracking setup, go through all your stories and make sure everything you need is documented in your current system.

NOTE: Okay. Now you can choose! And remember: the only thing that really matters is that the system you choose works for you!

PART III

WRITE YOUR SERIES

21

DOCUMENT YOUR WRITING PROCESS

I know, I know… folks who identify as pantsers like their freedom! I like room to move creatively in my stories, too. And while I love to just sit down and dive in, from an efficiency perspective, having even a rough plan in place before you start writing will generally save you a ton of time and energy in the editing stage.

You need to plot exactly as much as *you* need to work out the story issues before you dive in. Helpful, right?! Sorry. But this is one area where you need to figure out what works for you.

Through trial and error, I've discovered that for me, preparing to write is actually about getting to know my characters really well—things like their emotional wound, positive and negative traits, what they believe about the world and their families, and the stories they tell themselves about how they fit in their world and families.

Then I do a high-level plot, just a sentence or two for each scene, such as where it takes place and the key action.

Since I write romance, I'm generally alternating between the two main POV characters in a somewhat equal fashion. I try to write each scene from the POV of the character who has the most to lose in that scene.

That way I can still have the fun of being a "discovery writer" who learns all kinds of interesting things as the characters take on lives of their own, without wasting a whole bunch of time taking the story in a direction that ends at a brick wall.

Your goal as a strategic series author should be to write the cleanest first draft you possibly can since the less time you have to spend on edits and rewrites, the quicker you can get to the next book in your series. As a series author, time is of the essence since readers will be waiting.

Have a system for capturing ideas

As ideas bubble up, I open my Google Docs "ideas" file and jot down whatever little scraps of an idea I have. Sometimes these ideas are about characters, or a setting, or a situation, or an object that I think could be interesting. Until I figure out where the idea fits in my work-in-progress and how long the story wants to be, I usually leave those notes as a Google Docs file so that I can edit it from anywhere on any device any time I get an idea of something to add to it.

And for those of you shouting at me, "What about my notebook?!" I hear you. I feel you. I, too, am a devoted journal lover. I sketch and make notes and do little bits of brainstorming in my notebook all the time. And, after having lost track of too many story ideas on those pages over the years, I learned two hacks that help me stay stay organized and sane:

1. I keep a few sticky tabs in the front of my notebook and use them to flag pages on which I have ideas related to my series since my notebook catches all my ideas, not just series-related.

2. Before I move into focused writing, I transcribe all of those notes into my Google Docs file.

PRO TIP: Make sure you enable offline viewing of your Google Docs file if you're going to be some place without regular and dependable internet access. Any kind of document that is cloud hosted will work equally well here.

Document your process

Writing multiple books in a series is quite different than writing standalone books. You need a consistent voice, pacing, a series arc on top of your story arcs. You need to create devoted fans who come back story after story and who love your world as much as you do. And you'll need to track a million little details.

You also need to be able to replicate your writing process from book to book so that you can keep up with the demand for content.

As a series author, you'll also have the mixed blessing of readers who are addicted to your stories and are constantly asking, "When is the next book?" While this is certainly something to celebrate, it adds a layer of pressure since releasing new material regularly is a key part of a series author's success.

In order to estimate when your next book will be ready, in order to produce consistent content, and in order to *not* find yourself frustrated and written into a corner you can't get out of, you need a process. Ideally one that is efficient, fun to execute, and replicable so that you can do roughly the same thing over and over again with each book. This will save you time, energy and likely also money when you ripple the effects out over multiple books.

A lot of what you're going to learn in this book will likely influence your writing process for future books. But it's nice to have a baseline and know exactly where you're at when you're deciding whether or not to incorporate the suggestions in this book into *your own* process.

First, I'm going to give you a breakdown of my writing process, so you see what I mean and hopefully see how being a bit organized about this can be helpful and save you lots of time and frustration.

CJ Hunt's process for contemporary romance fiction

1. Jot notes in my journal and in Google Docs as ideas and inspirations trickle in from real life experiences, dreams, conversations overheard on the train—whatever.
2. Once the bits and pieces coalesce into something semi-coherent, decide whether the story warrants being a novel, a novella, or a short story.

3. Start a new Scrivener document using a template that I created with all my series settings and style guide pre-loaded. (I have three templates—one for short stories, one for novellas, and one for novels.)

4. Transfer all my hand-written and Google Docs notes about my plotting ideas, scene snippets, bits about my characters, etc. into Scrivener's research section.

5. Flesh out my main POV characters—their emotional wounds, goals, positive and negative traits, and assign them a central verb.

6. Use my "CJ Hunt Outlining Template" document to guide development of a more detailed outline, putting scenes into some kind of order and fleshing out the beats of the story, and the scene by scene verbs.

What the heck is a "CJ Hunt Outlining Template"? Yeah, I totally made that up.

I identified a few of my key tools, resources and books that are part of developing the story and characters for every book I write. Then I extracted the wisdom from them that I use every time I outline a new story.

Mine is a mashup of:

- Emotional wound for each main character from *The Emotional Wound Thesaurus* by Angela Ackerman & Becca Puglisi, plus
- *Romancing the Beat* story beats (Gwen Hayes) blended with
- Plot graph, pacing tips and character development

notes from *The Plot Whisperer* by Martha Alderson, then

- Chose verbs for each character and each scene, using the technique described in Damon Suede's *Verbalize.*

You can download my template from creativeacademyforwriters.com/resources/strategicseriesauthor. It'll be useful as an example, but your own template will be a mixture of whatever storytelling techniques, beat sheets, methods and genre conventions speak to *you* and go into *your* writing process.

Always remember, there is no *right* way to do this. There are just more or less effective versions of *your* way.

Your Turn

Ask yourself the following questions:

- Do you consider yourself a plotter or a pantser or a plantser?
- What is your current plotting/outlining process? Be specific about what tools you use, when you switch between them, and what you use each for.
- What is really working for you in your plotting and planning process right now?
- Is your process functional and replicable?
- Where do you struggle in your plotting process? Where do you get stuck? Is there anything you run

into that pulls you out of the writing and back into the planning while you're mid-draft?

- What areas of plotting do you need to gather more knowledge about?
- Is there anything you could add to or change in your planning process to avoid getting stuck in the drafting stage?

22

TARGET BOOK LENGTH

How long should your books be?

There is no real, *right* answer to this question. And, with the rise of digital publishing, there's no wrong answer either. Yay! Kindle now has categories for stories that are super short (1000 words or less), super long (200k words) and everywhere in between.

The answer to how long the stories in your series should be is: just as long as each story needs to be to fulfill readers' expectations about character arc and plot and to tell the story the best way possible. But there are a few guiding factors to consider when you're dealing with a series.

What do your fans want?

Do some research in your genre. It's fine to see a stat that says people are reading more short reads (under two-and-a-half hours or about 20,000 words long on Kindle) but if that is really only for mysteries and romance, and you write sci-fi, then that's not necessarily a good length for your work.

Should all the stories in the series be roughly equal length?

People like balance. While you can get away with the first in a series being shorter if it's going to be free, the ideal is to have all the books in your series roughly the same length. Readers get upset when they read two books in a series that are novel-length only to get a novella as the third in the series. Likewise, if your readers keep coming back for short stories and you drop a novel in your series, you'll undoubtedly upset—and probably lose—readers.

Size matters if you're planning to indie publish

When it comes to a series and word count, there are a number of specific factors you need to keep in mind. It may seem like you just write your book the length you want to write your book. But, since we're being strategic series authors, here we're leaving nothing to chance. And length is actually quite important when it comes to pricing, reader expectations and expected revenue. As well as scheduling your releases and your business planning and budget!

Book length and writing/release schedule

The reality of the indie publishing world is that every month after a book's launch, sales decline about 30 percent unless you're using ads to prop up sales and being super pro-active in your promotions. Even then, you can expect to see things slowing down on a month-by-month basis. Launching a new book is one of the most effective ways for authors to rejuvenate sales for their older series titles.

You need decide on a release schedule that works for you and will keep your readers' interest between releases.

For example:

- I want to release a full-length romance book every two months for the next year, in a new series. That's six books in twelve months—eight weeks per book from idea to launch.
- Each full length book will be 40,000 to 50,000 words (it's romance, remember).
- I know I need about four weeks in editing and preparing the book for publication, which leaves four weeks for plotting and writing.
- If I allocate one week for plotting, planning, fleshing out characters and any necessary research for their jobs, etc., then I'm looking at three weeks to write the story. Let's say each book averages 45,000 words, that means I need to write 15,000 words each week.
- Knowing I only want to work five days a week, I divide 15,000/5 and get 3,000 words per day as my target.

- I've written enough books to know that 1,000 to 1,500 words per hour is conservatively and consistently achievable when I am working from an outline.
- Looking ahead in my calendar for the year, considering the six book series I'd *like* to write, I can see I will not be able to complete a full-length romance in either October (conference season) or December (holidays with family).
- So, as a strategic series author, I adjust my goal to write four of the full-length books in my series and one short story or novella that I may use as my free book to introduce readers to the series.

But, what if you don't know how long it takes you to finish a book because this is your first one? Well, as long as you know how much time you have to work with and your writing speed, you can work your goals from the other side of things.

For example:

- You've decided you'd like to write a trilogy.
- You know you have thirty minutes each morning to write while you're on the train to work.
- You average 1,000 words per hour when you are working from an outline, so you can safely estimate you will be able to write 500 words per day if you write on your way to work. 1,000 words per day if you also write on the way home.
- Assuming you only write during those times, you should be able to produce 5,000 words per work

week. It will take you 12 weeks to write a 60,000 word novel. Or six weeks to write a 30,000 word novella.

- The editing, book layout and beta reader process takes about four weeks. This, of course, assumes you will hire an editor.
- With this information you can plan your publishing schedule. If your stories feel like full-length novels, you know you can write and publish three in the year. If your stories feel more like novellas, you can write and publish the three in six months.

Your Turn

- Using what you currently know about the stories and characters in your series, decide on a good target length for each of the books in the series.
- Track the time you spend writing and otherwise working on your books so that when you create your next publication plan you have solid information to work with.

23

WRITE YOUR BOOK

The most valuable part of the process is also one of the hardest things to do. And that is getting new words out of your head and onto the page.

Often when something matters greatly to us, we experience a high level of resistance to doing it.

What if it doesn't work the way we hope it will? What if we're not a good enough writer to do the story justice? What if no one likes it?

These are all questions that most authors face at one time or other.

The good news? There are many different ways to approach getting the words on paper.

Use every spare minute

I know several authors who have written entire books while waiting for things: kids, appointments, meetings, their favourite show to start, the kettle to boil for tea…

If you added up every time in the day when you had "just five minutes" before something else started, that time actually becomes something.

If you have a system where you're writing on your smartphone, then you can just pop open your Notepad or Scrivener file whenever you find yourself with a couple of minutes and get some more words of your story out of your head and onto the page.

Yes, you may only manage a few sentences in that five minute block but you'll be surprised how quickly they add up. And with such a short period of time that you're committing to the resistance is often much lower.

If you use the Pomodoro method of working for 25 minutes then taking a five minute break between tasks, you'd have an average of eight of those break blocks in a day.

How many words could you write in a day if you used only half of those blocks to write a few more sentences?

500 words at a time

Another approach is to commit to writing 500 words at a time. How long that takes you will depend on a variety of factors, but I can tell you from experience that it's possible to reach that word count in fifteen minutes or less if you hit your stride.

The only way to know how much time to budget is by testing it out for yourself. Sit down at your desk and write 500 words. How long did that take you? Great. Now block that amount of time every day… or plan to do it in five minute increments. It might only take you three, five-minute chunks to get it done. And if you write 500 words per day, you'll have the draft of an 80,000 word novel complete in less than six months.

Get up a half-hour early

Many people find that getting up a half-hour earlier in the morning is enough to make steady, forward progress on their manuscript every day. That 500 words we talked about can get written in that time.

Yes, you might be a bit more tired but often you'll fall asleep earlier to balance it out.

For many people, writing first thing is extremely efficient. The demands of the day have not yet taken over your brain, you're less likely to be interrupted by other people, and you'll feel great all day if you write your words first and have that win under your belt before you even tackle breakfast!

The commuter writing block

If you have a commute on transit or in a car where you're not the driver, then you can take advantage of that time to get some words down on the page. You could make really excellent use of those minutes if you have a portable tool to write with like a smartphone, tablet with a keyboard, small laptop—whatever works for you!

Write on your lunch break

We should all be taking a meal break mid-day, even at work. That is *your* time to use how you want. Depending on how long that break is, you likely have at least a few minutes you could dedicate to writing if that's the only time available to you. Even if you eat with co-workers sometimes, see if you can establish certain days of the week, or a certain amount of time that belongs to you and your writing.

For example, maybe you catch up with coworkers for the first fifteen minutes of lunch break and then you find a quiet corner somewhere to write for the other fifteen. Or maybe you spend your whole lunch break writing four days a week, then have lunch with colleagues on Fridays. If you are consistent with what you do, then it won't take long before that's the new normal and everyone will know what to expect from you.

Yahtzee Method

This is a great way to make progress, hit your goals and stay flexible with what you're trying to achieve each day.

Sometimes we just can't commit to the same word count or amount of time every day. The Yahtzee method allows you to check off what you can do each day.

For an explanation video and interview with author kc dyer who came up with this strategy, visit creativeacademyforwriters.com/resources/strategicseriesauthor. You can watch the video and download some templates to use as a starting place for creating your own Yahtzee sheet.

Don't break the chain / your longest streak

The key to building consistency and setting a new habit is to track your progress. Why is tracking helpful?

- You can't lie to yourself about how you're doing. Seriously. This is more of a problem than you likely realize. We tend to underestimate the frequency with which we do not-so-great stuff and overestimate the good stuff.
- The act of checking something off or getting a gold star or putting a circle on a day in your calendar or getting some points if you use an app like Habitica are all intrinsically rewarding, so finishing the thing actually *becomes* the reward.
- Most of us are innately competitive. You might be competitive with others (in which case throwing down a challenge to your writing bestie of who can get the longest streak might be helpful) or competitive with yourself. For example, you might set a series of goals with the intention of constantly working to beat your previous "high score" in terms of numbers of days in a row that you completed all your words.

Mind your mindset

And if none of these approaches work to get that story out of your head and onto the page, read *Scrappy Rough Draft: Use science to strategically motivate yourself & finish writing your book* by Donna Barker. It's all about helping you bust through those writing road blocks.

24

DETERMINE WRITING AND PUBLISHING ORDER

The order in which you write the books in your series can have a big impact on your launches and sales.

I can see the look on your face, and it could best be described as, *huh?* Because, obviously, we write the first book first and then the second book and so on. Right?

Well, in many cases, yes. But here's the thing: you are setting up to be a strategic series author. And assuming one of your goals is to reach as many readers as possible with your books, the order in which you write and publish those stories can have a big impact on your success.

C is for Cookie—and for Capturing new readers

One of the best ways to snag readers into your series is to have a free book—often a short story or novella—available to introduce folks to your characters and storytelling, to get them hooked and lure them into your world. The point, of course, of this free book is to get people to purchase, for money, another book in your series.

Marketers refer to this '"free taste" of what's available to purchase as a cookie.

Since you're writing a series, that cookie can be chock full of foreshadowing and hint-dropping to make people curious about events and characters in future books. It is a very powerful psychological tool. And, since this cookie is often the first thing a reader will "taste" of your writing, you want it to be shiny and sparkly and accurately reflect what readers can expect from you in future stories.

Think of the cookie like a really long book blurb that you use to hook reader's attention, draw them into your series, demonstrate the quality of your writing and then prompt them to buy the book that answers, "Well, what happens next?" That book will almost always be the first book in your series.

So, you want to make sure that nothing in this cookie is going to limit your ability to tell the rest of your story. For instance, what if you write the teaser book and part of the female protagonist's backstory, an event that feeds her emotional wound, is that her sister died when she was six years old. All is good until you reach the middle of book two when darn it all, this story would be so much easier to pull together if that sister had actually been a brother who didn't die but was kidnapped.

What I'm driving at is that many series authors write this series cookie—the novella or short story—*after* the other books are well underway. They write the first book late in the process.

If you're a linear, chronological writer

No problem. You gotta do what works for you, and you know how your brain works. Respect that. Write the books in the order they need to be written in.

But I strongly suggest that you not publish any of your books until you have at least a couple written. This serves two purposes. First, the one I refer to above of using the first book as a teaser into the series. The second relates to reader impatience once they find an author and a series they love.

Once you start publishing you need to give readers a sense of how long it'll be before your next book is released. In the current publishing landscape, making readers wait even three months is a long time to hold their attention. Heck, three *weeks* is a long time. Readers want to jump from one book into the next in a series, binging on an author once they find someone they love. It's Netflix binging with books.

And if you're indie publishing, there is no reason not to set yourself up for success by giving series readers what they want—great stories they can consume quickly, without waiting.

PART IV

PUBLISH YOUR SERIES

25

READY TO PUBLISH?

Making the switch from writing a series to publishing a series is a big, exciting, scary, wonderful leap.

My biggest regret? I wish I'd had more books stockpiled before I started releasing.

It's challenging to switch your brain between writing mode and launching/publishing mode. Even with over 25 books written and indie launched, I struggle to make time to get new words on the page when my promotion brain cells are active.

There's a lot going on when you cross over from writing to publishing. Like, a *lot*. It can be overwhelming and seem like every day you're climbing a mountain and learning something new. Which is exciting, yes, but also exhausting. Plus, there are only so many hours in the day.

The absolutely undisputed truth is that the best and smartest thing you can do to sell books is to write the best darn book you can. And the next best and smartest thing you can do to promote that first book is to write the one that comes next and ensure it's even better.

One of the main keys to success when writing a series is to have multiple books ready to publish at once or very close together. Momentum is critical when you're trying to get read-through.

Having multiple books available multiplies the impact of every dollar you spend on advertising, gives more weight to your presence in online stores, and leads to more sales as readers click the "Buy Now" button for your next book at the back of the one they just finished.

If you're early in your series writing career, it can be difficult to know just how long you'll need to write that second book, if things will change drastically from your outline as you write the next story, or if in writing books two and three you're likely to identify plot or world-building issues that need to change in book one. You may "discover" something about your characters or story that you wish you could change. Sadly, if book one is already published, you're stuck with what you've got.

At the very least, as a strategic series author, you'll have books two and three outlined in detail so that you know what happens next.

The exception? If you're planning to write a series longer than three books, you do not have to write all of them before you launch. But try to have the first three finished or very close to finished before you leap into the world of pitching or publishing. And ideally, have a cookie like a novella that introduces your world or characters.

What about writing more than one series at a time?

I would always suggest to new authors working on their first series, to focus exclusively on getting those first three books in that series out before they think about splitting their focus. But some authors actually like to have more than one series on the go—especially once they've been writing for several books.

Perhaps you have one long series that is popular with your readers, but you also want to explore other worlds and characters and stories. If that's what keeps you passionate about what you're doing, then write away! Just make sure you build up to that and are comfortable juggling your existing balls (aka your books) before you toss a few more in the mix. And I would caution you against having too many open series at once! This creates a lot of pressure on you from the readers (*When's the next book coming? When? When? When?* Now multiply that by x # of series!) but on the upside, it can keep you engaged!

Considering traditional publishing?

The same advice applies if you're planning to pitch your series to an agent or traditional publisher. They will be more likely to consider taking you on if you have a three-book series that is ready to roll, rather than a single finished book and the *promise* of more titles.

Having multiple books ready to go gives the publisher the option of bringing them out more quickly than a traditional one-book-a-year schedule.

26

TRADITIONAL OR INDIE?

Once you have your first couple of books written, you're going to be faced with a choice: Will you query agents and pitch publishers with a goal of traditionally publishing or will you indie publish your books?

Let's talk about the pros and cons of traditional versus indie publishing.

Traditional publishing

You sign a contract with a publishing house (usually *after* you secure an agent #**thisisnoteasy**, and they negotiate the details of a publishing contract for you). The publisher pays for all editing, production and publishing costs, and you get a percentage of royalties from all books sold. You may or may not get an advance against your royalties.

· · ·

Pros of traditional publishing

- They take care of cover design, editing, book layouts, and producing all the formats of books agreed upon in your contract.
- They set up distribution channels.
- You do not have to invest any of your own money in the process of publishing your book.
- Periodically (usually once per quarter or once every six months) you'll get a royalty statement that tells you how much money your book earned and how much is due to you.
- You'll get a cheque, if money is owed to you.
- You get the benefit of established systems, contacts, and usually a higher chance of being sold in bookstores if you're with a traditional publisher.
- You don't have to manage most of the business side of things.
- Your agent or publisher can often open doors for things like foreign rights sales that you wouldn't necessarily have access to as an indie.

Cons of traditional publishing

- Not all publishers can support you in the same way. Product quality, distribution channels and promo efforts may vary by author, not just publishing house.
- You don't have direct control over things like pricing, cover design, timing of book releases.

- You often don't have direct access to your sales reporting and revenue dashboards. This can make it difficult to get immediate feedback about whether or not your marketing efforts (including paid ads) are working.
- They can decide not to publish the next book in your series, and finding a new home for your partially published series can be challenging. This can leave your readers stranded unless you get back your rights to the earlier books and you're willing to indie publish them to keep them available.
- There are gate keepers and a lot of competition for a limited number of traditional publishing slots. Agents and editors are chased down at conferences, online and in grocery stores by people who want to be published.
- Traditional publishing moves very slowly. The amount of time it takes to find an agent and for that book to sell can be weeks or years. Once the book is sold to a publisher it typically takes twelve to eighteen months before that book will appear on shelves.
- Some contract clauses can be quite restrictive about what you can and cannot do with your work. (This is why it's so important to have an agent to help you with these negotiations.)

Indie Publishing

In indie publishing (or self-publishing) you are the publisher as well as the author. So you take on all costs, all decisions, all control, and you reap all the benefits in the form of royalties.

Pros of indie publishing

- You have complete control for every stage of the process and every decision made.
- You keep 100% of your royalties (keep in mind the distributors such as Amazon do take a percentage of the sale price).
- You control your writing and publication schedule.
- You can get from idea to market much more quickly than in traditional publishing.
- Once a book is published, if you want to make changes, you can.

Cons of indie publishing

- You have complete responsibility for every stage of the process and every decision made.
- You have to pay for everything yourself.
- You have to manage all the business side of things as well as the creative side, which can take away from writing time.
- It can be challenging to get your books into brick and mortar book stores or libraries.

What do you know about yourself?

Choosing whether to pitch your work or indie publish is about many different variables. We all have different reasons for wanting to be published. Some people want to write their magnum opus and just want to share their words with the world. Other people want to create a stable, full-time income. The book business is a bit of a roller coaster *(cough)* but there *are* ways to build a very respectable and solid income that evens out some of the uncertainty and change that are just part of the publishing industry if numbers aren't your thing.

If the very idea of being in business for yourself makes you break out in hives, then indie publishing might not be for you. At least right now. It is a business, and a phenomenal amount of work and learning.

But it *is* a sure thing. If what will make you happy is knowing that every book you write can be available for readers, indie publishing is a good way to go for you.

Another reason to indie publish is if the submission process is destroying your love of writing. It's hard to stay "up" if people are constantly turning down your books. Especially because it doesn't necessarily mean your book isn't good. It just means that they either don't have the right audience to sell it to, or it's not a good fit for them at this current time, or they just bought a book in that same vein and they don't want two competing titles to come out at the same time... or...or...or. There are a million reasons and yes, one of them might be that your book isn't ready for market yet.

Don't despair! There are editors to help you change that. A good editor is worth every penny you pay them and then some.

Ultimately, once your book *is* ready, the only person who can make the decision to **pitch** or **publish** is you.

The good news? You can always try pitching for a while as you write follow up books, and then if you don't get a deal and a few months or years have gone by, you'll have more books ready if and when you do decide to go indie!

Do I have to choose? Can I indie publish my series then sell it to a publisher?

Be aware that if you indie publish your series, unless it is very successful (by which I mean selling tens of thousands if not hundreds of thousands of copies), a publisher will not be interested in taking on an already published series. And if you *are* selling that many copies, you may not want to take the traditional deal being offered!

Why I focus on indie publishing—in my own series author career and in this book

I know a number of authors who have experienced great frustration when their publishers discontinued their series after the first few books had been published. They couldn't find a new publisher for future books because the publisher still owned the rights to the earlier books, and they couldn't get their rights back to the first few because they were still selling *okay*, just not well enough to lead to more books.

On the other side of the coin, I also have friends (very successful authors) who are trapped—locked into contracts for successful series they are no longer excited about writing, or are seriously stressed about hitting publisher-imposed deadlines for upcoming books.

Still other friends have signed multi-book deals with their publishers and are frustrated at the lack of marketing support they are receiving. But they are part way through a series, and still under contract, they have to stick it out.

I don't love the prospect of *any* of those realities. So I came into this process with a pretty good idea that I wanted to indie publish my books. Did it help that I had a background in publishing? Heck yeah, it did. But the biggest driver for me was **freedom**. I wanted to be able to follow the sales, experiment with what I was doing, follow the readers, and explore the world of my series in any way that would keep me passionate and excited about my writing life.

I'm also not very patient. So when I was looking at how long it could take to write, then pitch, then sell, then wait for publication… it was all just gonna take too long. So indie publishing is a perfect fit for me.

It may or may not be the perfect fit for you…

You do you

You are the only one who can make this choice for yourself. Personally, I love indie publishing because I can set my own schedule, I have complete control over my story world and all my rights, and I "get" to manage the business side and the design aspects of everything I do—both of which I love. I'm constantly learning new things. That's *heaven* to me. But if it sounds like *hell* to you, then you may want to explore other options (or, at the very least, look at hiring people to help you with the bits you really don't want to do!).

Your Turn

- Why are you wanting to publish your books? What are your specific goals for publishing your books?
- Make a pros and cons list of pursuing a traditional publishing deal for you and your series.
- Make a pros and cons list of taking the indie publishing path for you and your series.
- Do you have a clear idea of whether you want to pursue an agent/traditional publishing deal or indie publish the books in your series?
- Make a list of all the questions you would like answered before you make a decision.

27

PLOT YOUR PATH

Steps in book publishing

While everyone's path to publication will be uniquely their own, there are some stages that pretty much everyone will work through, whether you choose to pursue the traditional publishing route or decide to go indie. The main difference at each stage is whether you have control over the choices made, and whether or not you're footing the bill.

1. Write your book

This part you've got taken care of. (Seriously, you do.)

2. Polish your manuscript

You need to get your manuscript in the best possible shape, even if you plan to go traditional and you know there will be an agent and editor involved in giving you feedback and revisions before it hits the shelves.

This polish process may include hiring an editor, but you could also get this feedback by taking a critique class, sharing pages with a critique partner or having beta readers do a review.

3. Query agents / submit to publishers (indie authors skip this step)

There are a wealth of resources online and in print on how to find an agent and prepare your query. Typically, submitting manuscripts to editors of large publishing houses is done by an agent but there are publishers that allow authors to query them directly.

4. Work with an editor

Whether you're hiring an editor or working with a publisher's editor, your manuscript should be edited before it becomes a book.

Early stage editing is called developmental editing. This is focused on ensuring all the elements of the story, plot, character, dialogue, etc., work to tell your story in the best possible way.

Copy editing comes once the book is final. A copy editor focuses on finding typos, ensuring spelling is consistent, and fixing egregious grammatical errors. More on editing in **Chapter 33: Edit your books.**

5. Get your cover designed

For traditional folks, this will be taken care of by your publisher and the amount of input you get in this process will vary. For indie folks, you'll be researching cover designers, then hiring someone you know does great work in your genre. There's more on this in **Chapter 34: Design your covers.**

6. Interior layouts complete

This is the magical moment when your manuscript becomes a real book. You, or someone you hire, will use one of the tool options described in **Chapter 35: Prepare interior files**.

7. Publish your book

If you're indie publishing, you'll upload your book files (cover and interior layouts) to your chosen distribution channels, fill in all the metadata and descriptions, review a proof copy (print or digital) and then hit that publish button!

8. Launch your book

Once your book is live, you'll dive into all the launch activities like soliciting book reviews, sharing the news with your mailing list and connections, and generally spreading the word about your book.

9. Support your book

Once the launch is over, you'll enter an ongoing cycle of planning and carrying out ongoing promotions on your existing book while working on launching the next one.

In the sections that follow, we'll tackle the aspects of each of these stages that are specific to a series. If you're looking for the basics of how to indie publish, here are a few of my favourite sources of indie publishing information in the industry right now. These three sites are combinations of courses, books, tutorials, podcasts and loads of great articles and videos to help you. Much of it free.

- The Creative Penn by Joanna Penn
- Mark Dawson's Self Publishing Show
- Kindlepreneur with Dave Chesson

And of course, you'll find a ton of resources at creativeacademyforwriters.com/resources.

28

CHOOSE YOUR PLATFORMS

It may seem counterintuitive to consider the distribution stage before editing your books or designing your covers—but you need to know where and how you're going to sell your books (get them into the hands of your readers) before you make book design decisions.

Technical requirements for files are different on different platforms, options for books sizes and types of cover (hardcover, softcover, dust jackets, etc.) are different with different distribution companies, and knowing the guidelines of your distributors and chosen formats *in advance* will help the whole rest of your publishing process go more smoothly.

And because you are working with a whole series of books, you'll want consistency from book to book and as simple a process as possible to manage. So you want to get this right from the start.

Your first big decision is going to be what formats to publish your books in. Your options are eBook, print and audio.

Because each format has very specific considerations and tips, they've got their own section following this one.

Your second big decision is deciding whether or not you're going to be "wide" or exclusive to Amazon for each of those formats.

Going "wide" means your books are available on many different stores (Apple, Kobo, Kindle, Nook, etc.) around the world. There are certain types of promotions and opportunities only available to books that are published wide—getting on the *USA Today* bestseller list for example.

And distributors (also sometimes called aggregators) are the companies who can get your books into those different stores (Draft2Digital, PublishDrive, IngramSpark, etc).

"Platform exclusive" generally refers to selling your books through Amazon alone, although in theory you could go exclusive to any online store (like Kobo or iBooks). There are certain types of promotions and programs only available to books that are enrolled in KDP Select which includes things like the Kindle Unlimited program and the Kindle Countdown/free promotions on Amazon.

The major players in the indie publishing and distribution world are:

eBooks

- IngramSpark (wide)
- Draft2Digital (wide)
- PublishDrive (wide)
- Or you can upload your files directly to some of the individual eBook stores who have author dashboards including Kobo, Nook, Kindle Direct Publishing (Amazon), and Apple Books

Extra credit: Read *Killing it on Kobo* by Mark Leslie Lefebvre and learn about why you might want to go direct to Kobo, even if you use an aggregator/distributor for many other channels.

Print books

- IngramSpark (for hardcovers and full colour books with 2 colour quality options, wide
- KDP Print (softcovers only, black and white or colour, books are made available on Amazon, with option for expanded distribution to other stores if you choose)
- Draft2Digital Print (this service was in beta at time of writing this book, so details are not yet available)

Audiobooks

- Findaway Voices (Wide distributor for many stores including the three ACX supplies audiobooks to)
- ACX (Exclusively distributes to Audible, Amazon & iTunes)

Each distributor and store has its specialties, pros and cons —and there's no one right option. You'll need to decide on what platform or combination of platforms will work best for you, your goals, your tools/budget and your future series' plans. If you're not sure what to choose, go back to **Chapter 2: The KAREful Approach** and do that exercise again with your increased knowledge.

Some people will prioritize keeping the most royalties possible from each sale, which might mean uploading book files and managing accounts with many different distributors. Other authors will prefer going with the option that is the most simple and straightforward to manage everything from one place (or at least the fewest number of places possible!).

Likely you'll end up with a combination of outlets for your books—especially because you can choose to have some formats wide (like audio and print) and then make your eBooks exclusive to Amazon, if that fits with your overall strategy.

I actually use ALL of these channels (except ACX) for different purposes with my *Rivers End Romance* series, and for the *Creative Academy Guides for Writers* series.

eBooks

- Direct to KDP for Amazon sales
- Direct to Kobo if book is wide
- Draft2Digital for all platforms except Amazon and Kobo
- PublishDrive for the rest of the stores they supply, that Draft2Digital doesn't

Print Books

- IngramSpark for hardcovers, and the little pocket-size books
- KDP Print for large print books
- Local printer for author copies of print books for events

Audiobooks

I access Audible and other ACX channels via Findaway Voices but if I wanted to I *could* go direct to ACX for certain things. I just like to have everything for my audiobooks in one dashboard, and the folks at Findaway are awesome to work with so I'm happy to help support them by keeping everything in one place.

Your Turn

- What formats do you want your books to appear

in? (eBook, print, audiobook)

- For each format, do you want to be available *wide,* or *exclusive*?
- For each format, are you already using any of these distributors? If yes, make a list of all the things that are working great, and anything you'd possibly like to change going forward.
- What matters most to you when you're choosing distribution options—that you get highest possible royalties or that you can manage publication on all channels from a single dashboard, or something else?
- Which combination of options seem like the best fit for your desired formats and admin preferences?

29

SET YOUR BUDGET

The harsh truth in the publishing world is that selling the first couple of books in a series is really hard—whether you're talking selling to an agent or editor, or selling direct to readers. The more titles you have published, the easier it gets. To be clear, I'm not actually saying it gets *easy* at that point (seriously, if you're looking for easy, the writing and publishing world is not a good place to hang out) but it will get *easier*.

When you convince someone to give your first book a shot and they like it and just keep on reading their way through the series, you can effectively sell several books for each single new reader you attract. And if they like your books enough to keep on reading through your existing series, the odds of turning them into a superfan who will want to read everything new you produce are drastically increased.

Why does this matter and why are we talking about it in a section marked budget?

You're right to ask. But here's the deal:

Not only are you the *talent*… you are also the *money*.

For indie authors, you need to plan on footing the bill for all expenses related to writing and publishing the first few books in your series before royalties will start to cover those hard costs. And even longer until they start to pay *you*.

For authors seeking traditional publication it may take months or years to find a publisher for your books, and if you're a new author pitching a series, a publisher *may* want to see multiple books written before they agree to take on your series. You may need to work with an editor, coach or writing mentor while you learn your craft. You may be paying for access to tools or resources.

Most indie authors will tell you that it took at least four books before they got any kind of sales momentum and royalties. And even then, this will likely just pay for the costs of producing and promoting your books until you've published six or seven titles.

Yes, I can hear you arguing that any money you spend on indie publishing your book or polishing up your manuscript to submit to a traditional publisher is not only a tax write-off (because naturally, since this is a **business** you're tracking all your related expenses), it's also an *investment*. But I would urge you to think about that investment at first more as you would investing in your education. Not something you're depending on getting the money back out of. There will be a learning curve. You may not make your money back on each book. Some may do well and others less so. And some may take off and exceed your wildest expectations.

BUT. They might not.

And so you, the strategic series author, are going to set out with a plan to make sure that even if you have a sleeper hit that takes five years and six books in the series before it catches fire, that you've done this in a way that you can afford. You are going to plan to keep writing and publishing your series until that tipping point comes, without creating stress and strife and strain on your lifestyle or your family, no matter how long that takes.

Publishing is somewhere in-between buying lottery tickets and putting money into a pension fund as far as risky investments go. You can't win the lottery if you don't play. But in no way is winning the lottery a sure thing just because you buy tickets.

What costs do you need to budget for?

We'll tackle specifics of budgeting and pricing for print books in the next section, but for now let's look at the expenses related to the pre-publication stage of being a series author.

Remember, with a series your goal is to be running a financially viable business—not straining your family budget or your life. Knowing what costs are coming, and when you can expect to pay them, can really help you spread it out in a manageable way.

There are no hard and fast numbers on any of this. You can do everything yourself, with super minimal costs, or you can go all in and hire professionals all the way through. Publishing a book can cost anywhere from zero dollars to tens of thousands of dollars.

Personally, I think it makes a lot more sense to look at your budget and decide what you **do** have to work with, and then make decisions about how you're going to proceed based on that.

Here are some of the things that could cost you money along the way:

- Writing (tools, resources, *professional development* like conferences, writing groups, memberships)
- Developmental editing
- Copyediting
- Interior layouts
- Proofreading
- Cover design
- Publishing/distribution
- Author branding
- Website
- Mailing list
- Promotions (services and materials)

We're going to tackle these stages one-by-one, and we'll talk a bit about budget each step of the way. I'll always present you with a range of options from free, to DIY with paid tools, to paying a professional, so you're in a good position to decide what fits your goals, your timelines, your skill set and your budget.

Your Turn

- How much money do you have to invest in the writing and publishing of your book this month? What about for the next 12 months that follow? Write this figure down.
- If you don't have any wiggle room in your budget, think about what you could adjust to get even a small amount.
- If you have an annual budget that is separate from your monthly budget, how much can you afford to invest this year? Write that figure down.
- Now make a list of all the writing-related expenses you have already committed to. Things like conferences, editors, buying Scrivener, ProWritingAid and other helpful software, reference books, research fees, amounts for helpful apps, software and tools (you should have your inventory from the first section to refer to here).

There's a handy budget spreadsheet available from creativeacademyforwriters.com/resources/strategic-seriesauthor. I highly recommend you download it and make use of it now, so you know exactly what you have to work with and/or what your target is for saving!

30

EBOOK SERIES STRATEGY

Thinking about eBooks?

Some issues and choices that come up are specific only to eBook series strategy.

Are eBooks worth your time and energy?

Yes! They have no production costs beyond your file preparation, and they can be distributed worldwide and delivered directly to your readers. While the distributor of those eBook files will take a cut to manage all the sales for you (and some download fees to cover data costs in certain countries) you're still looking at a good profit margin. You have a worldwide market, and the potential for millions of readers. Once your manuscript is polished and your files are prepared, you can have your eBook published and available to readers world-wide in a matter of hours.

Exclusive vs Wide

When it comes to eBooks, maybe the biggest choice you're going to have to make is a choice between exclusive to KDP (Amazon) and "going wide." Print books aren't as restricted. What matters most is that you're consistent across your series. It's frustrating for readers to only get part of your series on the platform they prefer to read on.

KDP Select / exclusive to Amazon

Advantages

- You can participate in the Kindle Unlimited (KU) program, where you get paid for each page read by readers who pay a monthly KU subscription fee.
- When you do a price-break promotion through Kindle Countdown Deals program, you can retain better royalty rates than you would if you just changed the price.
- You can use Kindle Free Promotions.
- Kindle Owners Lending Library program (you get paid when people loan their kindle books to friends or family).
- Increased royalties for sales in select countries.
- Amazon's algorithms are good at working on your behalf to help sell books.

Disadvantages

- You cannot have your book anywhere else while it's enrolled in KDP Select.
- You are limited in frequency of price break

promotions—once every 3 months you can offer your book for a discounted price for 7 days, **or** free for 5 days.

- You are locked in for 90 days at a time.
- You cannot hit bestseller lists (like *USA Today,* etc.) if you're not available outside Amazon.
- You're missing out on some markets and countries where Amazon does not control market share.
- It's *much* more difficult to get a BookBub feature deal if you are exclusive to Amazon.

Things to note

- You sign up in 90-day terms. So you can sign up and then decide to change your mind. You can also go wide first, then remove your books from the other channels and put them in KDP Select.
- You cannot have a permafree book in KDP Select.
- You *can* still email copies of your ebooks to reviewers.
- A 10% sample of the book can be made available outside of the Kindle Store.

Going "Wide" and having your books distributed through multiple stores

Advantages and things to consider

- You can develop relationships with individual retailers, which may lead to additional promotion opportunities.
- Can qualify for "hitting a list" (assuming of course that you have stellar sales, on top of being wide!)
- Many authors report that income levels are more stable if you are wide, even through it takes longer to build up an audience.
- You can access audiences in areas where Amazon isn't present at all, or doesn't control the market.
- If something changes on one platform, you're not "all in" and vulnerable.
- More potential readers, and if you have books in multiple formats then the cross promotion of different formats can be very effective.

Disadvantages

- You don't get access to the KU page reads program and compensation.
- You don't get access to Amazon's other promotional programs.
- Amazon controls the majority of the market share in the US, which for most people is their primary market.
- Discoverability on Amazon, AMS ads effectiveness and author rankings may be negatively impacted by your book not being part of the KU program.
- Building up a readership can be harder/take longer on channels that are not Amazon, because they do not have the same algorithms driving search.

Preparing your interior files for publication

Although you can just upload a Microsoft word file to most sales platforms where it will be converted by their tools, I recommend you prepare your files using your own tools first, so you get it looking exactly the way you want it. The interior of your ebook will look best (and work best) if you use Vellum (Mac users, or with MacinCloud if you're on a Windows machine), or Draft2Digital's free formatting tools.

- .mobi is the preferred file format for kindle
- .epub is the preferred format for everywhere else

Preparing your cover files for eBook

eBook cover files are quite straightforward, since they don't require the "full wrap" that print does. You only need the front cover. You'll want to check the requirements for cover size on whatever platforms you've chosen—it should be the right proportions to display nicely in the available space, and you'll also want to make sure it's a high enough quality (pixel ratio) that it looks clear, and not fuzzy. More on this in **Chapter 34: Design your covers.**

eBook series consistency

For eBooks, it doesn't really matter how long your books are from a cost/practical perspective, but it is good to have at least some consistency within your series.

For example, if you're doing a series of short reads, then you might want to try and keep them all consistent at ten thousand words, so that readers know what to expect, and all of the stories fall into the same short reads categories length-wise.

Or if your series strategy involves pushing hard to build your KU reading audience, then longer books are going to net you better results. More pages = more revenue!

You want to make sure all the books in your series have a cohesive and coherent look as far as covers and interior design. It should be clear they belong together, and with a series, people are likely to be reading one book right after the other. They're going to notice if you're not consistent!

Do you need ISBN's?

Yes, best practices indicate that each eBook version of your book should have its own ISBN. One for .mobi (Kindle) and one for .epub which will be used everywhere else. Some eBook distributors will assign an ISBN for you if you don't have your own. Just be aware, that they are then the publisher of record in all the databases. Personally, I recommend that you get your own ISBNs if at all possible.

Series bundle pages on Amazon

Your series may qualify for a series bundle page on Amazon. This means your whole series will be displayed on one product page, and as long as all your titles are available there will even be an option for people to one-click purchase all the books in your series bundle. If you want to explore this option, make sure you check out the rules and regulations for series bundle pages to ensure your series qualifies.

If you are writing a linear series, where the books are meant to be read in a specific order, then this series page makes sense. It will list the books in the reading order you want them to be read in (you assign a book number in the series when you set up your book on KDP) and then people can actually one-click purchase your entire series if all the books in the series are available on Amazon.

Some downsides? At the time of writing, the Series Bundle help page on KDP says it can't handle numbering outside of whole numbers. For example, if you later add a prequel to your series you can't assign it number 0 and still have it linked on your series page. Or if you have a novella in between two full length titles you can't number it 2.5 or 3.2 or whatever. (This is when it pays to have mapped out your series titles and numbers in advance!). However—rumour has it that functionality will be available any day now!

Another consideration is if you have a whole bunch of titles linked in the same world, but they don't have to be read in a specific linear order, then you technically don't qualify for a series page.

How to get the best of both worlds?

Because ALL my *Rivers End Romances* are set in the same world, and linked in multiple ways, I do want it to be easy for folks to find all those books together. But they aren't linear, and they don't fit the guidelines for a series page.

Plus, I don't always release the stories in a "logical according to the chronological reading timeline" order, and sometimes I add bonus books, novellas and stories into the middle of what I had planned. I know, some of you are either cringing or jealous right now. But hey, it works for me to keep the freedom level high and my passion and excitement for the series alive so no judging my creative chaos in this area.

The solution? I break the stories into mini-series, and then each of those mini-series gets a series page of its own. For example:

The MacAllisters of Rivers End series has four novellas in a series that are best enjoyed in linear order. They were published in chronological order, and are all available so you can see the single click to purchase them all button on the page. And if/when I add additional stories that fit into this family's tale I can add them to the series. That way, readers see everything together on one page.

Your Turn

- Review the list of Pros and Cons for being exclusive vs wide.
- Brainstorm a list of any additional reasons you might have for preferring one over the other (for example, you are located in a country where Amazon doesn't control the market share).
- **Feeling ready to make a decision?** Are you

wanting to go exclusive to KDP or wide to a variety of online eBookstores?

- **Not ready to make a decision?** Gather more knowledge—ask authors you know, do some reading online, and then pick something to start.
- Does it make sense to include your series (or a portion of your series) in a series bundle page on Amazon?

31

PRINT SERIES STRATEGY

Thinking about print?

There are a handful of things to think about that are specific to having your series in print format.

Is print worth your time and energy?

This is a tricky one. And as usual, the answer depends on your goals, your budget and your genre.

If your readers prefer print copies of books (such as children's books and books aimed at older readers) you might find that having print books is a key part of your sales strategy.

If your marketing strategy for your series includes targeting libraries to stock your books, then you'll definitely want print copies available.

If you're running a lot of paid ads on your series, then having multiple formats for people to choose from may increase the effectiveness of your ads.

The good news is that with print-on-demand technology you don't need to commit to big print runs and large expenses to make your books available in print.

Preparing your interior files for print

In fact, the interior of your book will most likely have a print ready PDF generated by the same software you used to convert to eBook (Vellum or Draft2Digital's formatting tools, for instance). If you prepped the interior files for your book using Microsoft Word, be aware that you will want to choose KDP Print as your distributor as at the time of writing this book, IngramSpark doesn't accept print PDF's generated using Microsoft Word.

Preparing your cover files for print

What you *do* need is a "full wrap" version of your book cover. This means a cover that has a back and spine as well as the front you use for your eBooks. Ideally, you'll get the base design created when you get your eBook covers designed (and then just tweak your spine width when you have your final page count).

You'll need to know what platforms you're publishing on since, for instance, KDP Print cover templates are different from IngramSpark templates. They also have different trim sizes and use different paper—the thickness (or weight) of the paper changes the spine width which impacts your cover design.

This may sound intimidating but as long as you use the templates that your chosen platform provides to put your final cover files together, it all works.

Standard print sizes and choosing your formats

How do you choose the right trim size and formats (hardcover or softcover?) for your books?

Best practice is to look at all the possible channels you might want to use (KDP Print, IngramSpark, and a local printer for your author copies, if you live outside the USA) and then compare which sizes they can accommodate.

Then look at your software (Draft2Digital layout tool or Vellum) and compare that list of standard sizes to the standard sizes on the print platforms.

You want to pick a size that *both* your software and distribution platforms accept for large scale distribution.

What if you want to be a special snowflake?

Ahem, yeah—I did this. I really wanted my novellas to be in print. And I really wanted them to be pocket-size books on their own instead of bundling them together in a larger format. So I picked the smallest format available on IngramSpark (4″x6″) and then manually laid out the files using Adobe InDesign. If you're a badass with InDesign and want a distinctive format for whatever reason, have at it. I have to say that I've had more attention for my cute little pocket books at events than I ever could have predicted. Are they a pain in the behind and labour intensive to prep? Oh, yes they are. Do I regret that? Not at all. Just make sure you've willing to go to the extra trouble and expense if you want to do something similar.

"Future You" is depending on "Today You" to make this process as easy as possible for them. What seems like fun now might not be quite as nifty when you're on book #17 in your series.

Print book series consistency

You don't have to decide before you start writing exactly how long and how many pages your book will be. But it is good to have a rough idea.

You want to make sure that whatever you are setting up as the print publishing standard for your series is something you can stick with over time. The readers who will want to collect every one of your books in print will also want to line them up on their bookshelves and have them look like a set. Like a glorious group of things that belong together. We want that hum of completion, the feeling of checking off all the boxes when we see them sitting there all shiny together on the shelf.

You want to make sure all the books in your series have a cohesive and coherent look in size, shape and in design. It should be clear they belong together.

Print cost and impact on pricing and royalties

The length of your book and how many pages it takes to tell the story impacts your printing costs. The number of pages is determined in large part by your word count but is also impacted by font size, gutter size, and the size you've chosen for your book. Amazon and Spark have calculators to walk you through figuring out your print costs based on all the variables.

You want to find the sweet spot between a book that feels hefty enough to justify the price you're charging and that is inexpensive enough on the print side that you make a little money from each copy sold.

For example, when I was trying to decide what formats to do my *Rivers End Romance* novellas in, I looked at a compilation of all four of the MacAllister stories. They are novellas, so I thought they'd be good all in one book. But the collection has to be quite expensive to justify the print costs.

In the end, it made more sense to do super cute little pocket book-size print editions (through IngramSpark) and large print editions (through KDP Print) of all the individual novellas.

- If you know you're aiming for a 20,000 to 30,000 word novella, or 30,000 to 50,000 word short novel, that information will help decide on trim sizes.
- And if you're going to tackle an epic fantasy series with books that are all 100,000 to 120,000 words, then make sure you choose your book size, font

size and price point accordingly. You need to make sure there are royalties left for you at the end of the day, and print costs get expensive when you're dealing with lots of pages.

And one more thing: you want to run the numbers on what price to charge for your shortest book and your longest one so that you can figure out a coherent pricing strategy for all the books in your series.

Tools to help you figure out royalties

If you're trying to decide if printing books will be worth your while from a financial point of view, do an online search for <IngramSpark Royalty Calculator>, or <KDP Print Royalty Calculator> and see what it comes up with for your books.

Get a separate ISBN

Your print version of your book will not share an ISBN with your eBook. This would be like assigning twin sisters the same social security number. Not cool.

They are different products, and have their own identities out in the book world.

First, check to see if your chosen distributor has free ISBNs available or if you need to supply them.

In Canada, ISBN's are free (I know, we're spoiled in so many ways). In exchange, we just have to submit copies of our books to the National Archives.

If you live in a country where ISBN's cost money and you don't have the cash, there is an option to use a free ISBN service. However, be aware that the publisher of record will be the company who owns that ISBN. It will not be your name or the one you've chosen as your indie publishing company name.

And, if you're paying for your ISBNs, you can usually get a better deal when you buy a block. As a series author, this is a good investment as you'll need a unique ISBN for each format of every book in your series. If you publish a trilogy in hardcover, paperback, ePub, Mobi and audio formats, simple math tells me that you'll need 15 ISBNs.

Set-up fees and fees for updates

When you're choosing the company to work with for your series, consider the fees for file set-up and making changes to your files.

Some platforms, like IngramSpark, charge a fee to set up each book ($49 at time of writing), and also have a charge each time you make a change to your files (like when you update your *Also By* list and your back matter). They also charge an annual cataloguing fee for each title. If you publish a lot of books in your series these fees can add up quickly.

You need to build those fees into your budget, or join an organization that will give you access to a coupon code so you don't pay those fees. Just make sure that your system would still be sustainable if that coupon code disappeared!

Be aware that if you're new to indie publishing it might take a few tries to get your files right. Each try could cost you, depending on the platform you use. If you think you're going to be making frequent changes to the books in your series or will be publishing a ton of titles, you might be better to go with one of the options that doesn't charge for setup or updates.

My print strategy for my *Rivers End Romance* books uses a blend of tools.

1. I set up my large print editions through KDP Print. They are a standard size so I can use Vellum to lay them out. These titles are easy to add to my KDP dashboard which lets me track sales in the same place as my eBooks.

2. I set up my special snowflake pocket book editions using IngramSpark, and because of their non-standard size I use InDesign to prep those files. I am a member of the Alliance of Independent Authors because it saves me on set-up fees and update fees.

3. I order author copies for signings and events from a local printer in my home province of BC. It's a little more expensive per copy, but for anyone living outside the USA, the exchange rates on the US dollar, the shipping costs for international shipping and surprise duty fees (not to mention the extra time it takes to get those books through customs) means that I can pay more per printed copy and still come ahead. And, I get the added good karma points for supporting a great local business.

Print books, bookstores and deep discounts

You may be thinking you'd like to sell print books in bookstores. It's quite challenging as an indie author to do that. Do some knowledge gathering of various authors' experiences if this is a goal for you. It's not impossible, but it is a lot of work. And you're going to be playing in what has historically been the sphere of traditional publishers. This is where they (and their deep pockets and well established connections) tend to clean house.

You'll need to set discounts for online stores and brick and mortar locations to buy your books from your chosen distributor.

If you go through KDP Print they'll set those discounts for you—at 55%.

If you go through IngramSpark, you'll choose how much discount off the retail price you're willing to give the stores that will sell your books. This is usually between 35-55%. Then, you have to decide if you're willing to allow returns or not. Allowing returns is a risky proposition, that can get expensive, but is pretty much required if bookstores are your primary goal.

And an extra consideration when it comes to a series in print—will the bookstore stock your whole series or only your new release? Will readers buy book two, three, four, or five in your series if that's all the store has? Or will they find a series that has book one available for them?

I don't want to rain on your bookstore fantasies, but if you are going to make this a priority, I encourage you to do some serious research first before you dive in.

The distributor you choose will have information in their help sections to guide you on setting prices and discounts that work for their customers.

Your Turn

- Do you want to do print copies of your books?
- If yes, why do you want to do print editions?
- Do some estimating of costs: How much will it cost to have the files you need for print produced? How much will it cost to set them up? How much can you sell each book for? How much can you expect to earn per copy sold? (Use the distributor's royalty calculators for this)
- What discount level will you offer if you're going through IngramSpark?
- How many print books would you need to sell to recover your costs?
- Are you targeting online sales of your print books, or going after library sales/bookstores?
- Will you pay for your own ISBNs for all the books in your series or opt for the free ones (if you are not a Canadian author)?

32
AUDIOBOOK SERIES STRATEGY

Audiobooks are another publishing format and the popularity of audiobooks is on the rise.

Audiobooks are very different than publishing print and eBooks. While there is a bit of crossover (the story, for one) they are very distinct products that appeal to a different audience. As such, there's a whole other way of doing things and connecting with readers if you're diving into the audiobook pool.

In fact, there's enough to say on this topic that I'm going to tackle it in another book in this series called *Strategic Audiobook Creator*. But for now, I'll give you a super quick rundown on the ways you can produce audiobooks, and some things to keep in mind if you're dealing with a series so that you can decide whether or not this platform is going to be part of your strategy.

How do you get your books into audio format?

If you're going to do audiobooks you have four choices.

1. You can pay to have your book produced and then you own 100% of the rights and royalties.

2. You can enter into a partnership/royalty share arrangement with a narrator and then you'll split your royalties with them—usually 50/50. The advantage with this approach is that you don't have to outlay any cash to get your audiobook produced.

3. You can narrate it yourself. I really don't recommend this unless you're a professional voice actor/audiobook narrator. Not only is it a steep learning curve, but if you're spending a ton of time on converting existing stories to audio, you're not spending that time writing the next book in your series.

4. You can license the rights to another company that makes audiobooks. Someone else handles *all* the details. You negotiate an advance and then receive royalties once that advance earns out.

How much does it cost to produce audiobooks?

Costs to produce an audiobook generally are in the range of $150 to $600 per finished hour of audio. This equates to roughly 9000 words for one finished hour. Narrators range in price quite drastically. And your genre expectations will determine how important it is for you to have a "big name" narrator versus someone newer to the scene, therefore more affordable.

If part of your strategy is having multiple products released in a reasonably short period of time, that will be much more expensive if you're writing really long books.

If your series is composed of shorter parts, you might find audiobooks to be a great way to build an additional revenue stream with manageable costs, and someone else handling production.

Many eBook platforms sell listeners "credits" which they can then choose to "spend" on an audiobook of their choice. But if you only have one credit per month, and you're a savvy, thrifty listener you're going to want to get a nice big chunk of listening time for your credit. Which means short little audiobooks like mine aren't going to be your first choice.

However, there is the option to make your audiobooks available to library patrons, and the libraries can buy them outright (at what is usually a higher than normal price) or they can pay you a percentage of the cover price for each listen of your audiobooks that a patron makes. Cost to listeners = $0. Revenue to you varies depending on your prices you set—but I can tell you I have found this to be one of my most lucrative royalty streams for my audiobooks.

Then when you've built up a few shorter products, you can bundle them into longer collections of your whole series or mini-series of shorter pieces, and the listeners on platforms with a credit-based system will start to get on board because they can get the whole bundle for one credit.

Audiobook lessons

Here are a few tips based on my experiences over the last 18 months with audiobook production for my *Rivers End Romance* series (aka, here's where you learn from my mistakes!).

Be flexible with your timelines and launch plans

Why this? At the time of writing, you can't just set a release date for your audiobooks, which means that if you are trying to plan a simultaneous release in multiple formats it's a bit...*challenging*. And audiobooks can take weeks or even months in the production phase—so you need to make sure you're flexible with booking release timelines and promotions. Ideally, you'll have the production phase of your audiobooks finished well before you schedule your book's release. And then, when you do push that publish button, timelines for different distributors vary widely.

Do the whole series in audio at once with the same narrator

If you want the same narrator to do your whole series (and you don't have an open-ended, long running series) consider getting all the books recorded in a set period of time (even up to a one-year period).

Why this? You'll ensure consistency from book to book, you'll have all your audio assets to work with at once, and you can choose if you want to release them separately, all together as a boxed set, or both.

Consider using different narrators for different books in your series

Why this? If you have the kind of series where there are different main characters in each book, you may want to have different narrators for different books so that you can adjust as time goes on without worrying about keeping the same narrator on contract for years. This is especially important if you don't know how many books there will be, and if you want to keep your options open. Often, once narrators get more popular and established, their prices go up. You may or may not be able to afford to keep up with the rising production costs as this happens and it's nice to have options without it being jarring for your fans.

Sign a contract for a set number of books (ideally the whole series) in advance

Why this? If you know how many books there are in your series and you'd like them to all be the same narrator (i.e. a five book mini-series, where the main character is always the same person) then you may want to negotiate a contract for all the books in your series over a set period of time to guarantee your narrator's availability and also the production costs. Signing a contract in advance is one way to secure this.

· · ·

Release your whole series only as one big audio boxed set

Why this? If you have limited time and energy for promotion, or you want to go big on promoting just one product, then you can release your whole series as one big boxed set. There are lots of benefits to this approach:

- It will prevent you from losing listeners along the way if the books aren't all out when they start listening to your series.
- You can control the listener experience from start to finish and make sure they listen to them in the order you want.
- You can focus all your promotional efforts on one product (reviews on single titles are separate from reviews on boxed set products... and it can be hard to get people to post in both places).
- Your sales ranking on one product is easier to maintain than on several individual ones.
- Your boxed set will appear as better value for the folks on the credit systems, and you're more likely to get higher volume through those channels with longer works.

Wait a few months before releasing a boxed set if you have single audiobooks out already

Why this? Don't release the boxed set of your whole series until a decent amount of time has passed since you released the last standalone in your series. Six months was the time gap suggested to me by several different sources. Otherwise, you risk upsetting your loyal listeners who bought individual audiobooks at full price.

Wait until your book has been out at least a few weeks or months before you add audiobook production to the mix

Why this? Especially if you're new on the series writing scene, you may find it helpful to wait on audiobook production until you iron out all the little bits and pieces in your process. You want your book content perfect, and you want to make sure that you've addressed any issues your readers have identified with your story before you add audio into the mix because it's expensive to change audio files. You also want to make sure you have an audience for your series before you take the expensive step of converting your stories to audio.

No, these are not hard and fast rules

I've broken all of the rules (some by accident and some on purpose) but the biggest thing to keep in mind is that a strategic series author will mitigate financial risk, while investing in their series development. All while making sure the water is deep enough before diving off that cliff face.

Your Turn

- Do you have the money to invest in having your audiobooks produced? Or would you need to go with a royalty share option?
- Do you like/listen to/feel passionate about creating audiobooks?
- Do you have an established readership already for your series?
- Do you have several titles ready to be recorded?
- Do you believe audiobooks are a key part of your strategy as far as building an audience?
- Make a list of pros and cons for doing audiobook versions of your series titles.
- Now ask yourself if waiting six months, or twelve months before you dive in would remove most of those *cons* from your list.
- If you decide not to dive in immediately, make some notes on at what point you would like to revisit your decision and review any new knowledge/options?
- If you do decide to dive in—how do audiobooks fit into your larger strategy? How much time and money do you have available to dedicate to growing your audience of listeners?

33

EDIT YOUR BOOKS

In many ways editing for a series is similar to editing a standalone book. You will likely want to include developmental editing, copyediting and proofreading stages as part of your process.

The exact ways you go about these steps will depend on your budget, your goals, and your readers' expectations. Sometimes, if you have a truly exceptional story and characters that yank your readers into your series and keep them turning pages, you can get away with a few typos.

But your target should always be to produce the most professional, polished work that you can possibly manage.

Strategies to increase accuracy

Be faithful about updating your systems for tracking your characters, settings and timeline.

This will help you start off with accurate information in the first place.

Create and follow an editorial style guide.

You'll want to be consistent about things like American vs Canadian or whatever country's spelling you're going with, whether you're spelling out numbers (four vs 4) and all kinds of other consistency issues. You'll want to know this for yourself, and it really helps to make sure you're not missing things if you (or your editor) can run down the list and confirm the details. Add this to your "series bible" (your system to track settings, characters and events) and make sure it's available to yourself and your editor.

Hire a professional editor.

Wherever possible, I recommend people hire a professional editor. If you can't afford to have a professional help with all three stages (developmental, copyediting and proofreading) then do whichever of the pieces you can afford and will get you the most bang for your buck.

For example, if you're a newer author you might really need the feedback on the story side of things and then you can use beta readers and editing software like ProWritingAid to help you polish it up. For more experienced authors who are confident in their storytelling craft, it might make more sense to have an editor do the final proofread.

Hire an editor for certain parts of the project and then learn from their suggestions.

If hiring an editor is not something you can afford to do on every book, or for your entire book, then at least have someone edit a sample from your book or help you set up your editorial style guide so that you can do the best possible job of self-editing that you can.

Strategies to maintain consistency

In a perfect world you will use the same editor across all the books in your series—this assumes, of course, that you've found a good one.

If you can't use the same editor, then make sure you're using the same editing process and editorial style guide on all the books, so that difference in editorial style is minimized.

Strategies to decrease cost

Do multiple self-editing passes through your manuscript

You want to present the cleanest manuscript possible to your editor to save their time and your money. You do this by making a checklist for yourself of what you're looking for, and doing multiple editing passes through your manuscript before you hand it over. Your checklist will depend on what issues you've identified in your writing and story. But some common questions writers ask as they do self-editing passes include:

- Do you have enough conflict (the answer to this is generally **no**!)? Are you being too nice to your characters?
- What can you do to boost the conflict?
- Are your characters' goals, motivations and flaws clear to the reader?
- Are there any "info dump" sections you need to cut or information you could redistribute for maximum effect?
- Review the dialogue. Do all your characters sound the same or can you tell who is speaking even without dialogue tags?
- Does your story follow a clear arc?
- Does your protagonist change and grow throughout the story?
- Do they contribute to solving their own problems?

Use editing tools to polish

There are software programs like ProWritingAid and Grammarly that will analyse work and point out errors to you. These are much cheaper than paying a professional editor by the hour to correct every small issue in your work. This is a great way to polish as much as you can before you submit to your professional editor, and improve your skills along the way.

Use critique partners, beta readers and ARC readers

These readers can help you catch errors and issues, clean up your work and save editing costs. As these are generally volunteer positions, be sure to temper your expectations. While some of these volunteers are highly skilled and know their story stuff, you can't expect they will always be available when you need them, or that they will be able to catch everything.

Reflect and evolve with each project

You're going to be learning as you go. We all are. I still am and I've indie published over 15 stories in my *Rivers End* series alone. Every book you write and publishing, you should be getting better. Your writing will be getting stronger, and you will be catching more issues before you get to the "paying an editor" stage. If you are constantly making improvements, your editing process will become more efficient as well.

34

DESIGN YOUR COVERS

Decide on your promotional tools

I can hear you thinking… *wait, am I in the wrong section?* And if not, *why can't I just choose my promotional channels after my covers are designed?* Well, here's the catch: many advertising platforms and promotional services have rules about what can and cannot be on book covers that participate in their promotions. The rules change from time to time, so this is not an exhaustive list. It's just to get you thinking. What are some things that can limit your options for advertising?

- Weapons—there are rules about how they can be held, what directions guns may be pointed, who can be holding them, etc.
- Blood—doesn't even have to *be* blood, it can be something that *looks* like blood.
- Anything related to drugs —so if you have a

medical thriller, a syringe may not be your best option!

- Sexual suggestiveness—romance authors, you can have loads of freedom on your covers for any books you're *not* going to run ads on—but for the keystone books in your series that you may want to buy ads for, review the policies carefully before you pin down that cover.
- All kinds of other things we've likely never thought of.

Because you are a *strategic* series author, you are going to make sure you look up the current guidelines for your genre and chosen platforms as part of the research you do *before* you hire a designer, so that you are certain you haven't removed a promotional avenue before you even get going. Even many experienced book cover designers won't know the rules for advertising. Their job is cover design. It's *your* job to share the relevant business information about restrictions with them and protect your investment.

Be specific about what your goals are for your series covers

In order to help the designer do their best work, you want to be prepared to answer all their questions and provide useful information—but still leave them enough room visually to create something even more wonderful than what you've pictured in your mind.

A valuable exercise is to pick three to five examples of covers you love from the top 100 books in your genre and explain what you love about those covers. Then, find two or three examples of covers you don't like and what you don't like about them. Be specific in your evaluation of other book covers but leave your designer room to do what they do best.

In addition to finding those love and hate examples, you will want to have a package of information ready for your cover designer (and, heck, preparing this will also help you recognize the *right* designer).

What do you need to know before you dive in?

- Genre conventions you need to adhere to.
- Image restrictions based on your marketing and advertising plans.
- Existing branding elements that need to be tied in such as a specific colour palette or author font.
- The connecting element between the books in your series so the covers can depict this.
- Any reference pictures you think will help your designer capture the tone you want to set, the way your character looks, the location of the book, or any significant object that is in the story or series.

Indie Pub: Research the designer

Engaging a cover designer for your book series is a big commitment. It's an important working relationship and will have a huge impact on the success of your books. I'm not saying that to scare you or add pressure, just to call attention to the fact that it's important to do your homework.

What to look for in a series cover designer?

- Their experience creating other covers *in your genre.*
- Their experience creating *series* covers.
- Their stability (Have they been around for years or is this a new business?).
- Their references (Contact some of the authors they show in their portfolio and ask if they would choose to work with the designer again if they were starting over. You can find most authors via the contact forms on their own websites.)
- Their price point on a single cover, several covers, eBook covers, print covers, 3D mock-ups, a cover image with no text (for creating banners and promo images) and anything else you think you might need.
- How long they need to deliver finished covers.
- How many cover mock-ups they'll provide.
- How many revisions they allow on the mock-ups before they do the whole set.
- At what point do they start charging by the hour for adjustments.
- How quickly they reply to your query emails.
- How clear they are in their communication.

Decide on your level of investment

It's rare these days for books to keep the same covers for more than a few years—particularly in fiction. Non-fiction trends don't seem to change quite as rapidly, but it's still likely that your book will change covers in its lifetime.

You need professional-looking covers that speak directly to your target readers, clearly communicate your genre, and that fit with the other top-selling books in your categories on Amazon and elsewhere.

But assume that the trends will change within the next two to five years for what "the cool authors" in your genre are doing and that eventually you'll need to refresh your covers to stay current.

Weigh your budget for your covers against the assumption that this will likely be a recurring cost.

You will want to go with the best you can comfortably afford at the time. Then when you scale up your sales and have money from sales to reinvest, you can level up accordingly for the next go round.

Get covers designed as a series set

This is a great way to save waiting time, as it's common that good cover designers get booked out months in advance, or sometimes take breaks or leave the industry all together. If you don't want to be waiting in line for future covers, or risk having to switch designers part way through your series, then getting them all as a set will save you from potential delays.

Most designers also offer discounts when you book multiple books in the same series at once. Once you pin down the look on one or two sample covers, it takes less time to ripple that out over the rest of your books. You can always price out the covers you need for your series in advance, and then start saving towards that while you're getting the first few books written.

Doing them at the same time will also help guarantee that you get the same look across all of them. Covers purposely designed as a series set will generally have a more uniform look, they'll fit together better and you'll get the chance to see up front if the image choices or the typography choices will be an issue.

That said, if you expect it will take you longer than two to three years to release all the titles in your series, I recommend you get only the books you expect to have published in this timeframe designed.

Many authors I know actually get their covers designed before they write the series. That way they can generate some excitement with readers for the whole series, and have a clear map to lay out visually what books are coming and how they all fit together so people know what to watch for.

Especially if it's your first series, having the visuals for the whole series can also help to give you something to populate your website with.

Personally, I *always* do covers first. It helps me to see the book as a finished product (I *just* have to fill in the blanks between the cover pages. Hah!). But kidding aside, it's really motivating to see that book cover up on my monitor while I'm working on the book. And it helps keep me on target, as well as giving me something to email readers about. Marketing experts say you need to see something seven times before you buy it, so if you can get some of those cover impressions in while you're talking about the writing process of the book, then when your launch email goes out it'll already be familiar to readers.

PRO TIP: If you're going to produce audiobooks, you will likely want to get your audiobook cover designed at the same time as the other formats. This is generally a bit cheaper than going back to your designer later, and guarantees you won't end up waiting if they're backed up.

Boxed set covers

If you're planning to eventually offer the books as one or more boxed sets, consider getting the designer to make you a boxed set cover at the same time. Many designers have add-ons like promotional images, 3D cover images and boxed set covers that you can request when you place your cover orders. If you're a Photoshop user, you can create these yourself easily using templates from Covervault.com.

Be deliberate with your titles

Pick your longest and shortest book title to be the ones that the designer starts with when they're prepping samples. That way you can see how both extremes work on a cover and adjust the design to account for all the options. And the closer in length and construction you can make the titles in your series, the better.

Choose images wisely

If you're choosing images or sample character models from a stock image site for your cover designer to use, look for options where there are a number of different positions and poses for your character.

If you're doing a custom photography shoot to get original images for your designer to work with, it may be well worth your time to do some advance planning around other poses (or even other models) that would work for future books before you start. It's often much cheaper to do one longer shoot with costume or prop changes and to have another model or two added to the shoot than it is to book a completely separate shoot for each book cover.

Secure your image licenses directly

If you have an image of your main character or a setting on your cover, purchase or obtain the license directly so that you can use it in promotional materials, on your website, in book trailers, etc. This also comes in very handy if your designer is no longer available and you have to hire someone else to complete your series. Instead of having to start over and rebrand everything to get consistency, or settle for a "close enough" kind of match, you'll have the pieces you need to work with in order to do that correctly, and without violating any licensing agreements.

Secure your font license directly

Some designers have amazing font collections, which is a benefit to you when they use them on your covers. But if you're working with a specific budget, you may want to request that they not use any font that costs more than $X to license since you should own your own font license to be super consistent with your branding. In almost every case, there will be something similar to an expensive font that is available for free or at a reasonable cost. Cover designers won't always think about this since they just use the tools they've got access to, so it is worth asking.

Consider a templated cover design

If budget is an issue, and you have decent Photoshop skills (or even just a good eye with stock photos) then you can work with someone who will design you a template. Then maybe you change the colour, and the typography on each book and substitute the image for something new. *Et voila!* A new cover that's pseudo DIY.

Series cover case studies

I've pulled together a few different examples of series covers for you, and then highlighted different elements in each set so you can see illustrations of some of the things I've been pointing out as options.

CASE STUDY: Jonas Saul (Thrillers)

https://jonassaul.com/

This case study of Jonas Saul's thrillers was chosen to show you how easy it is to pick out which books belong together in the same series, and which are stand alone titles. Two of these things are not like the others... I bet you can tell which ones without me pointing it out. This is what strong series branding does.

CASE STUDY: Jeremy Mathiesen (Y/A Fantasy Adventure)

Author Jeremy Mathiesen has a fantasy adventure trilogy with illustrated covers. You can see how the artwork behind each is original, but consistent. And the backgrounds and colours are all part of a clear colour scheme, which combines with the consistent titling element and the same author name font across all the books.

Kindle Edition
$0.00

Kindle Edition
$4.99

Kindle Edition
$4.99

CASE STUDY: JP McLean (Addictive Fiction)

https://jpmcleanauthor.com/

These covers are a great example of using a recurring character in different settings. Although there's a broad colour palette, the recurring font and positioning of the titles make it clear that these books belong together as a series.

CASE STUDY: Cora Seton (Contemporary Romance)

https://www.coraseton.com/

Bestselling contemporary romance author Cora Seton makes an excellent case study on stellar branding both within each of her series, and across her various series. Take a look at the samples that follow (there are loads more covers on her website) and see if you can identify why I picked these books as an example for you.

The Sheriff Catches a Bride

When county sheriff Cab Johnson gets a hunch, he's learned to trust it, and his hunch tells him Rose ...

The Cowboy Lassos a Bride

Jake Matheson loves everything about ranching the Double-Bar-K, except for his father's controlling nature. It's bad enough the ...

The Cowboy Rescues a Bride

Ned Matheson is sharing a house with the woman he loves, but he can't kiss her, or even touch ...

The Cowboy's Secret Bride

Millionaire Carl Whitfield has set his sights on small-town chef Camila Torres, but she won't have him until he ...

The Cowboy's Outlaw Bride

It's Turners vs. Coopers — and all is fair in love and war ...

The Cowboy's Hidden Bride

The feud between the Turners and Coopers is all tied up, and the race for the Founder's Prize is ...

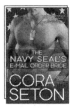

The Navy SEAL's E-Mail Order Bride

Mason Hall, Navy SEAL, knows all about difficult assignments, but his current mission is one for the record books. Not ...

The Soldier's E-Mail Order Bride

Staff Sergeant Austin Hall has a brilliant record in the Special Forces — except for one disastrous decision that cost his ...

The Marine's E-Mail Order Bride

If Gunnery Sergeant Zane Hall wants to save his family's ranch, he'll need to fix up the buildings, ...

Issued to the Bride: One Navy SEAL

Marry — or else. Navy SEAL Brian Lake is out of luck. Going rogue on his last mission landed him on ...

Issued to the Bride: One Airman

Airman Connor O'Riley doesn't believe in love. But when he crosses into a warzone to rescue a downed ...

Issued to the Bride: One Sniper

Sniper Hunter Powell thought he lost everything when he took the rap for a crime he didn't commit in order ...

Why did I pick these as examples?

- It's clear at a glance what genre we're dealing with —contemporary romance, some military, and some cowboy.
- The titles are consistent lengths and use consistent wording within each of the series. They also indicate the trope that's featured in each book (which is how many romance readers pick their books).
- The author name is a consistent font with consistent placement across all the series
- Good, solid author branding as well as series branding.
- While the only connection between navy seals and cowboys in this case might be their six-packs (or 8

packs?!?) you can clearly see that all of these belong to one author, and see which ones belong together in a set thanks to the consistent backgrounds.

Your Turn

- What promotional tools are you planning to use for your series? (Note: even if you're not running ads now but you might want to later, include them in the mix so you leave those doors open for future you.)
- Find three to five examples of series covers in your genre that you like and make notes on why. (Ideally, pick these from the top 100 books in your genre category on Amazon.)
- Find two or three examples of series covers in your genre that you *don't* like and make notes on why. (Ideally, pick these from the top 100 books in your genre category on Amazon.)

35

PREPARE INTERIOR FILES

Your options for preparing the interior of your books is going to depend a bit on what platforms you've chosen and what type of hardware (computers) and software you have access to.

Make sure you check with the distribution platforms you've selected to make sure that you can use the software you've chosen. For example, at the time of writing, print book interior files prepared in Microsoft Word are not accepted by IngramSpark. You don't want to get to the uploading stage and find out it doesn't work.

Some options of layout tools

Draft2Digital (free)

One of the tools Draft2Digital has available for free on their site is a layout tool. You upload your Microsoft Word document (or other format) and then it converts it into a variety of formats for you—including print. Even if you're not publishing through Draft2Digital you can download those formatted files and use them on any platform you want. There are several built-in templates to choose from and you can get a certain amount of customization.

Microsoft Word ($)

While it won't work for all platforms, many platforms can either use Word documents—or convert them to something they can use to set up your eBooks. If you're setting up interior files for print books, you'll want to download provided templates (KDP has these) for your book size, and then prepare your layouts in those templates.

Vellum ($)

This is the unicorn of layout softwares. It's amazing and I can't even express how much I love it. It can prep eBook and print layout files in a fraction of the time it used to take me to do layouts using InDesign and a variety of eBook conversion tools (plus HTML) for the eBooks. The challenge is that it's made for folks using Apple computers. If you're not a Mac user, don't despair. You can still use Vellum—you just need to use some work arounds such as MacinCloud.

InDesign ($$)

This is a more complex software to use, and it's a bit more labour intensive on the file preparation side as well. But it was the industry standard for book layouts for many years, so if you're comfortable using it and/or wanting to do a "non-standard" size of print book that Vellum can't handle then it's worth learning. Many professional layout folks will be using this if you hire someone to layout your book. It's got the most flexibility of any of the tools... but it's also one of the more expensive to buy and time intensive to learn.

Hire a professional ($-$$$)

The professionals you're hiring could be using any of the options you see above to prep your book for you. When you're getting estimates from them, be sure to clarify which tools they will be using, and ask whether or not you will be able to keep your source file as well as the finished product so you can make changes to your book files as needed. If you want to update your files every time you publish a new book in your series you do not want to have to pay someone else (and wait for them to do the work) every time.

I really, *really* encourage you to invest in the software that will make this step easy and pleasant for you, and invest the time to learn to do your layouts yourself. This will save you money over several books, give you the freedom to make tweaks to your front matter/back matter/sneak peeks anytime you want, and often you will catch things you'd like to change on previous books that someone who is not the author wouldn't think of.

For example, you're doing the layout on your current book and decide at the last minute to add a new call to action at the end of the last chapter, or tweak the wording just slightly to be more effective. Not only can you make these last-minute changes, you can ripple it out to the rest of the books in your series without waiting on anyone else or having to pay for their time.

Make yourself a layout template/style guide

It's not only the covers you want to be consistent from book to book. It's a nice reading experience if someone is going to read all your books in a row if they have consistent layout features inside as well.

I know from experience that keeping this consistency is harder than you'd think if there's a significant gap between formatting different books in your series. You don't want to have to go back and figure out what your settings should be.

PRO TIP #1: Create a "blank book" template in Vellum, Word or InDesign that you can load each time you layout a new book file. Populate it with your standard front and back matter for your series.

PRO TIP #2: If you're using the layout tools in Draft2Digitial or Vellum, you can screenshot your settings and keep that in a document so you can quickly scroll through it and compare it to the new book you're setting up.

Your Turn

- Gather information on each of these options and test out free trials wherever possible.
- Which of the file preparation options are possibilities with your hardware and your skills?
- Which of the file preparation options are possibilities with your budget?
- Which seems like the best fit with the platforms you have chosen for distribution?

36

CRAFT BOOK DETAILS

When you're publishing a series, your metadata and your front and back matter present an excellent opportunity for you to make sure it's as easy as possible for readers to find all the books in your series. Your choices here will also help to guide them to the next action you want them to take—whether that's reading the next book, joining your mailing list or becoming part of your private readers group.

Front Matter

Also By page

This is a common feature that you find in books where authors list all the titles they have published. If you have more than one series, this is especially helpful for people deciding what to read next, or to help them understand how those pieces fit together. Even better is when those book titles are live links to the Buy page for those books.

PRO TIP #1: Use GeniusLinks ($) or Draft2Digital's Universal Book Links (free) to make those links automatically correct themselves to the purchaser's local Amazon store (GeniusLinks) or use the free Universal Book Links to take people to a single page where readers can choose from all the online stores where your book is available. Bonus? You can see how many people are viewing and clicking that UBL link.

PRO TIP #2: Some authors create a page on their website that lists all their books with live buy links (organized by reading order, and/or by mini-series) and link to that page from a call to action in their book. That saves them having to change the links in their published books. You can use a phrase like: *Click here for a complete and up-to-date list of titles by AUTHOR NAME.* This is a particularly good idea if you're paying someone to do the formatting of your books.

Introduction / Dear Reader

Often series authors will include a bit of an introduction to each book in the series. This helps to flag for the reader where it fits in relationship to the other stories they may have read, and can also help you call their attention to other books that fit with it or share a timeline to help them get the best reading order and avoid missing out on something you want them to read as part of the story experience. It can also help you connect with the reader in what feels like a direct or more personal way, which can help them feel comfortable with you and increase the chances they will accept an invitation to connect with you through one of your calls to action at the end of the story.

Calls to action

1. To buy the next book in the series

Your number one goal with a series is likely getting read-through. You want to make sure you cover your bases a few ways. One is going to be your Also By page which we already covered.

You're also going to want to put a bit of a teaser **right at the end of the last chapter** with a short call to action. Why right at the end of the last chapter and not in a section of its own? Certain eReaders (ahem, Amazon Kindles) will have a popup that displays the second the person hits the end of the last chapter. Not everyone realizes that there's more to come after that if you just close that popup window. So it's good practice to make sure you let the reader know what's what!

For example, the following appears on the last page of the last chapter of *The List (The O'Donnells of Rivers End #1)*:

> *Curious about Marcie and Patrick? You guessed it— they get their own story and it's up next!* **One click CLASS ACT (The O'Donnells of Rivers End #2)** *now and dive right in.*
>
> *Want a sneak peek? Keep reading.*

Which brings us to the second way to get people into the next book in the series. Ever been hooked in by an author who puts the first chapter of their next book at the end of the current one? Yep. Works on me pretty much every time. By the time I get to the end of that first chapter I'm hooked and want to know what happens. This is extremely effective—assuming of course that your first chapter of the next in series is engaging and carefully crafted to hook the reader right from the start. Naturally, yours will be. So don't forget to include a little preview at the end with another call to action option at the end of the sample that says something like:

> **Click here** *to grab the rest of this book and find out what happens in (book title) or to (character names).*

PRO TIP #1: Some distributors don't allow links to other bookstores in your files. The way you can get around that is by using Universal Book Links to use one centralized link for everyone, or by creating files that are specifically uploaded to the different channels. For example, all my Kindle books have links that go right to the Buy page on Amazon. But for wide books, I always use a Universal Book Link.

PRO TIP #2: What if your next book isn't up on pre-order and/or you don't have a polished sample to include? Write a short teaser statement and then make your link go to a landing page where you collect the reader's email so you can notify them when it does go live. For example:

> *Things heat up for Marcie and Patrick in CLASS ACT (The O'Donnells of Rivers End #2). It's coming soon, so **click here** if you'd like to be notified as soon as it's released!*

2. To join your mailing list

Make sure you include an invitation to join your mailing list. Remember, with a series this is a great place to put some of your world-building stuff, deleted scenes, and earlier books or short stories to use. You can lure your readers in with some behind the scenes info and exclusive goodies that only your VIPs get access to.

PRO TIP: Include this call to action in a couple places. Many authors place it at the front of the book and again near the end of the book. Depending on what e-readers and platforms your book is being enjoyed on, sometimes readers don't always see all the front/back matter.

3. To join your community

If you have a private reader group on Facebook or through Patreon or another service, you will want to include an invitation for your readers to join you. And in an eBook, you can make that a direct, live link so it's a one-click process for them to sign up. You can have one group that is thematically titled for your series so you only have to manage one space. For example, I have the Rivers End Bookclub. Readers can hang out there and interact, and when you need new ARC Readers, or when you're announcing a new release it's just one more way to get that news out in front of your readers.

Some folks question why you'd want both a mailing list and a reader's group. But lots of people will unsubscribe from your list as time goes on, or maybe your emails get caught in a spam trap. If you have a reader's group as well, you're more likely to be successful in having your info reach your readers.

As great as having a reader's group is, you also really do want to be collecting email addresses since groups on platforms you don't control (ahem, Facebook) change group rules from time-to-time and suddenly nothing works the way it used to. You need to have confidence that you'll always have some way to reach your readers.

4. To follow you on other platforms

You'll also want to make sure that somewhere in your reader journey and calls to action that you're pointing out what other platforms you're on. In addition to the usual social media channels, you may also want to highlight any writer-specific profiles you have like Goodreads or BookBub. That way when you have new releases it's one more way to keep in touch. Often the best place for this call to action is with your "About the Author" page info.

Sales pages and book listings

Blurbs

Your blurbs (about the book copy on your sales pages) are an opportunity to mention that this book is part of a series and to give readers a heads-up about recommended reading order if that will improve their reading experience. And if you're looking to get your book included on a series bundle page, then you'll need to include something to indicate where it fits in your numbered series. For example, you can put a sentence like this right into your book description:

Class Act is book number two of seven in The O'Donnells of Rivers End mini-series.

Or you can include something like this at the end of the blurb.

The O'Donnells of Rivers End Series

1. The List (Selina + Connor)

2. Class Act (Marcie + Patrick)

3. Charmed (Darcy + Finn)

Editorial reviews

If you have reviews by other authors then make sure you get these on your product pages. On Amazon this will mean using your Author Dashboard (not from your KDP account) to get those added to your book listing. And remember, one of the benefits of having blurbs from other authors or reviewers who enjoyed your books is that if they are phrased as the series—you can use them on all of your books in that series. This can be a great way to populate that section of your book pages right from the first day your book is live, rather than having to wait until blurbs for that specific book come in.

. . .

Categories

In some cases, it will make sense to have every book in your series in the same categories. If you have a linear series, with the same characters, and a story that is being told in three parts—then yes. You'll want people to find all three books if they find one.

But if you have a looser linked series in a larger world, perhaps one where reading order is not so critical, then you might actually benefit from having different books in the series show up in different categories (if, and only if that is appropriate to what that book is about). Having multiple entry points into your series can expose you to more readers.

The way categories are handled on different platforms varies. Some let you pick two, some three—and if you're "in the know" on Amazon (which you are now!) you can actually request to be added to up to 10 categories.

Here's an example:

Book #1 in my O'Donnells series fits well in categories like:

- Contemporary romance
- Small town/hometown romance
- Holiday romance
- Interracial/multi-cultural romance
- Kindle Short Reads

Book #2 in my O'Donnells series fits well in categories like:

- Contemporary romance
- Small town/hometown romance
- Interracial/multi-cultural romance
- Second chance romance

The benefit of having some categories that cross over and some that are specific to each book is that I've created many more opportunities to connect with readers and draw them into the series. The cross-over categories ensure that things are similar enough to be coherent as a series.

Keywords/key phrases

When you're choosing keywords or search terms for your book, the strategy is similar to that of categories. You will likely want to have some similar keywords and phrases from book to book across your series, and others that are specific to the book.

Think of ways people might relate to your book, and what may draw them in. You could focus on details like:

- Theme (redemption and family tragedy)
- Character types (strong female heroine)
- Setting (small town in western Canada)
- Genre + tropes (second chance romance with a happily ever after)

Your keywords are more important than you may realize— and are not limited to single words. You can put whole phrases in like I have above. Dave Chesson has a fabulous set of information about how to choose your keywords on his Kindlepreneur site. I highly recommend you work through some of his tutorials.

I personally find Dave's Publisher Rocket ($) tool to be very helpful in choosing keywords and categories for Amazon, and had a great bump in downloads on my books when I redid the keywords using the information from the tutorials and the tool in combination to help me choose the best options. But if you're looking for a free solution, you can test keywords using the autofill option on Amazon. Go there and start typing in part of a keyword phrase, and see what it suggests you fill it with. Those are things people are already looking for.

PRO TIP: This will work best if you are working on a browser with a Virtual Personal Network or VPN (browsers like Opera have this installed automatically) so that it's not just autofilling with things *you* have looked up.

PRO TIP: If you're publishing through KDP, your keywords can actually be chosen in such a way that they will get you automatically added to certain categories. If you'd like to find a list for your genre, Google "Kindle Category Keywords List for (insert your genre)", and see what you can find.

37

SET BOOK PRICES

There are a number of factors that come into play when you're thinking about the price of your books. What people expect to pay for your length and genre of book is the primary one. Second most important factor is the cost of producing that product. You need to price at least somewhat competitively, as well as cover your costs and ensure that there's something left over to cover your time.

For eBooks, that means factoring in the cut your distributors keep. For print books, print and shipping costs become relevant. We talked about minimum prices as they relate to some of the production cost issues around this in the eBook series strategy and print book series strategy sections. Now, there are a few more things to think about.

How and where are you publishing?

If you're being traditionally published, you probably won't get any input at all about your book price.

If you're indie publishing, then the platform you're on will have an impact on what average prices in each genre look like.

For example: Kindle readers are programmed to look for lower prices and deals. While readers on other platforms (like Kobo) might be more used to buying books at non-discounted prices. You'll need to research your platforms and the audience of your genre. The best way to do this is by looking at comparable authors on each of the platforms where your book will be listed and then taking note of where the average prices are falling. Also take note when you see a sale or discounted price, of what the regular price point is for that book.

What are your goals?

Much like other areas of publishing, your pricing model is going to depend on what you are trying to achieve.

If your goal is to attract as many new readers as possible to your book one in your series, then you may want to go as far as permafree on the first book in series, with a goal of converting as many readers as possible to purchase your boxed set (or at least the following books in series).

If your goal is to run ads on your first-in-series and use those to scale up your sales, then you will not want your first-in-series to be free. You'll want to make sure it's priced competitively enough that people click on your ads and purchase, but not so low that you are losing money on your ads. Ideally you want your ads to pay for themselves via sales. And then some…

Pricing to entice folks into your series

Let's say your goal is to offer one book permafree, and then have the next one at a slightly lower cost to get people hooked into your series before you ask them for a full price purchase of book three and all the titles that follow. That is a solid strategy.

If you only have three books you may be reluctant to give away the first one and discount the second. It may make more sense to focus your energy on getting readers into your series via ads, or if it's a linked series, through one of your other products, and then having the first title at reduced price and the other two full price.

Sometimes, it's hard to convert those free readers into paying readers, so know your own goals—higher levels of exposure vs higher likelihood of read-through on paid books vs profits on the books you do sell—and then make decisions from there.

Is this a cookie to get people to sign up for your newsletter?

You can kind of straddle the line on this if you make your first-in-series a lower cost than the others on your various distribution channels, and then you offer it for free to folks who sign up to your mailing list via your website or through a BookFunnel promo. As long as you're not exclusive to Amazon, this doesn't violate any rules—at least none that I'm aware of at the time of writing.

Are you going to put your books in Kindle Unlimited (KU) or sell wide?

If you plan to publish wide, which means make your books available on all the platforms (Amazon, iBooks, etc.) you just decide on a fair price for your book, post it, readers pay it and you collect your royalties. End of story.

But if you are going to put your book in KU, length becomes relevant. This is why:

- If you have a retail price of $4.99 for your eBook, you will make roughly 70% ($3.49) of that amount for each sale that happens through Amazon.
- Now if your book is available through Kindle Unlimited, you will be paid for the number of pages readers in the KU program read, as well. The amount authors are paid for each page read is $0.0048 per Kindle Edition Normalized Page (or KENP) at the time of publishing this book.
- If your book is 60,000 words, then for each KU read you will make $1.64 (assuming the reader finishes your book). That means you're sacrificing revenue per read, for the hope that you'll see much more volume through KU.
- But what if your book is 120,000 words long? Then you'll be making $3.28 per book that is finished in KU. That's virtually the same as the $3.49 you'd

make if it were purchased at $4.99. And more than
you'd be making at $3.99 price point…

So that's partly what you have to think about. Do you
know where readers of the genre you write buy their
books? Are you in a genre filled with KU readers? Or do
your folks still buy their books outright? Chances are
good, the longer your books are the better you are going to
do being part of Kindle Unlimited.

Another consideration if you're pricing to encourage KU
page reads, is that KU readers love a bargain. So you may
want to actually price your books a little bit higher so that
it feels like they're getting a great bargain if it's better for
you to get paid in page reads, rather than outright
purchases.

Strategic bundles and boxed sets

Before you create your boxed set, think about the price
points you will likely want for these. If you're selling on
Amazon, you want to price between $2.99 and $9.99 for
maximum revenue return, since any price below or above
that range only gives you 35% royalties, while inside that
range you make 70% in royalties.

If you're wide, then you can be more flexible with pricing
your boxed sets.

For example, let's say you publish wide. You may want
one boxed set of the entire nine book series that you can
sell for $29.99, so you capture that one sale and increase
the likelihood that your readers will work through all of

your content. But for Amazon sales, it might make more sense to break it into three boxed sets of three books each, which you would sell for $9.99 each. That way you're still keeping 70% of each sale instead of 30%.

The math:

30% of $29.99 = $8.99 to you

70% of $9.99 x 3 sets = $20.97 to you

Even those of you out there who aren't fond of math, can get behind *this* kind of math, yes? Doing this quick and easy calculation lets us see clearly that it's the same books and the same amount the reader pays to access those books (okay, actually 2 cents cheaper for option 2!). But by being strategic in your bundling you're going to make an extra $11.98 per complete series sold.

PRO TIP #1: Remember that a boxed set is a separate product, which will need its own reviews.

PRO TIP #2: You will also need to consider that your individual book sales may drop as readers buy the boxed set instead of the single books. Why do you care? If you're running ads on your books, part of your ads strategy (and cost) is based on the ranks of your books. If you are running ads on single titles in your series, be aware that a boxed set could actually decrease the effectiveness of these.

Strategic bundling to increase KU page read revenue

If you're going to put your bundle in Kindle Unlimited and take advantage of page-read revenues, then you'll want to make sure that each individual book is *not* published wide. Review the rules around exclusivity and make sure that every book in your boxed set qualifies.

Multi-author boxed sets

Often the reason for doing a multi-author boxed set is quite different from bundling your own products together. Again, how you handle this all boils down to *why* you're doing it.

Attracting new readers into your series (free or $0.99)

Sometimes authors band together and make a permafree or $0.99 boxed set which they all promote. Generally, these are most effective if they are themed and/or quite specific to a certain genre or subgenre.

For example, if you have a boxed set of contemporary romantic suspense novels set during the holidays, and if everyone in the boxed set submits either a standalone or their first-in-series, then it can be a great way to attract new readers, and it's a great price point to run promos on.

Trying to hit a list ($0.99 price usually)

Many authors will band together with folks from their genre and put together a multi-author boxed set of their first-in-series which they may make available wide for

$0.99. This seems like a ridiculous bargain, but if you're making a run at the *USA Today* bestseller list, this was historically one way to do it. Because your price is $0.99 you can get on loads of deal lists, you have many authors to share the cross promotion and boost the size of the audience, and it feels like a steal of a deal for readers.

Which price is right?

The verdict? Yeah, you were hoping I'd tell you the surefire way to nail this, and I didn't. I really am sorry. But that just isn't how this works. Like everything else about publishing, there's no "right" way—just the "right way for you."

Hopefully, after you work through these Your Turn questions you'll have a better idea of what makes sense for *you* and *your series*. And remember—the beauty of having multiple books that all play together is that you can test, and trial, and evaluate what works and what doesn't. And then you adapt and see how those changes impact your sales. You're in this for the long haul. You'll have plenty of chances to "Get it right" for you with each new book you release in your series.

Your Turn

- Check out the bestsellers in your categories—what

are the most common prices in each of the formats you are considering?

- If there is a range of prices, look at the book details to see what factors are influencing this. (Traditional/indie, length, position in series, new release or backlist, part of a current promotion).
- What patterns do you see?
- Find five other series in your genre/subgenre on the bestseller lists for your category, on the platforms you've chosen.
- What patterns do you notice about the way those authors price different books in their series?
- What royalty restrictions do you have on the platforms you've chosen?
- What is the minimum you could price your book?
- What is the maximum you could/should price your book?
- Calculate your approximate royalty for each price point in between.
- If you've got one or more published titles, look back over your data and see what impact changing prices has had on your sales.
- Map out your tentative pricing schedule for the first few books in your series.
- Test it out, tweaking as necessary. Review your pricing prior to the release of each new book in your series.
- Re-evaluate pricing before each new promotional activity.

38

TRACK FEEDBACK AND CHANGES

Along the way, you'll likely discover things in your older books that need changing. And if you don't, your readers will point them out to you! Seriously. It's best to see this as readers doing you a favour and not focus on what's wrong. Because every tweak you make to get your book closer to perfection is just going to help you sell more books in your series and keep those readers happy in your story net.

And when those emails, direct messages or highlighted pages that someone helpfully photocopied and brought to a writers' meeting, or underlined in your print copy book and gave back to you (I kid you not) come in, you will have somewhere to track that feedback.

You're going to have the most momentum around your series at launch time. And ideally each new launch is going to scale that up even more than the last one. This is a perfect time to update the front and back matter in all your books, and also the best time to make those corrections your readers have so kindly pointed out need to be made.

You want your most perfect book possible to be what new readers are getting, and your older books to feed the success of your newer book with a clear pathway from one book to the next.

How can you track suggested changes?

I use Asana to track these suggested changes—as well as things I find that I want to change when re-reading. Asana is a free, cloud-based, project management tool.

I particularly like this because I'm able to make each book a project, put in the change requested as a task, and then break down all the formats of my book that need to be changed as subtasks so I don't miss anything. This is especially valuable when changes can't be made all at once.

For example, I can make eBook changes instantly, but I might do the changes to the print edition in a batch, and the audio changes might need to wait until I have the voice actor back in the studio for the next book in the series.

Or maybe I read a book by another author and love the way they handled their back matter. I will take a screenshot and drag it into the task description area and store all that together. Then, when I'm doing my next round of updates, I can include all the good ideas I've collected since the last batch.

Be sure that somewhere you have a record of which versions of each book you have and what distribution channels they are set up through since you will need to change all the versions in all the places.

Case study example

Title: Silver Bells

Change: reader found a typo in chapter three. "Kitten" should be changed to "kittens."

Attached file: screenshot of issue from reader to show location on iPhone.

Formats to review and revise:

▫ eBook (KDP)

▫ eBook (permafree, ePub via D2D)

▫ Softcover print book (KDP Print)

▫ Large print book (KDP Print)

▫ Hardcover print book (IngramSpark)

▫ Audiobook (Findaway Voices)

If you don't have a project management program or notes tool, or a spreadsheet or Word document where you gather information like this, even just having a notebook with a page for each book will do the job. The best system is the one you use 100% of the time.

Your Turn

- Create a system and a spot to capture all feedback about changes needed to your books.
- Make a note of all the files and formats you will need to update, and where each of those files has been or will be distributed.
- If you already have notes in various places (maybe sticky notes in your print copies of existing books?) map all those changes into your new system. If you're storing these in email folders, extract all the changes required and put the information into your system.
- Review your published files and make sure your current working file (the most up-to-date one) is very obviously labelled. With a date (year, month, day) so they auto sort for you.
- If you have files that need updating use your most recent files and the changes you have bookmarked to test out your new system, and make any adjustments you need so that it works for you. Don't forget to update the file name with the new date.
- Set a date on your calendar, or a to-do item in your task management program that will pop up to remind you when it's time to update your files next.

39

UPDATE YOUR BOOKS

When you're writing a series, every book you create, every item of promo material, every bit of research you do can be re-used, re-purposed and re-cycled when you have a new book out.

Which means everything you create becomes part of your catalogue of assets for your series.

We talked a bit already about managing your files, file naming conventions, backing things up and tracking reader feedback.

Now let's look at a few more ways to maintain your assets and make sure your books are always kept refreshed and up-to-date.

Update front matter and back matter

You won't only be correcting errors. Each time you update your book files is the perfect opportunity to make sure the following things are working as hard for you as they possibly can, to lead your readers from the current book in your series to the next one:

- New formats of the book (added to your copyright page)
- Complete list of all your other books, both in this series and elsewhere (added to your Also By this author page)
- Buy the next book link (added at the end of the last chapter)
- Sneak peek sample to pull your reader into the next book (added after the last chapter)
- Your author bio and social links (added after the sneak peak sample)

PRO TIP #1: You'll get the highest consistency and best chance of having a great reader experience if you prep the changes first and then update *all* the books in your series by copying and pasting that content so they are the same with your front and back matter. New readers will be coming into your series all the time and if they burn through all your books in a short period, that extra attention to detail in keeping the older books up-to-date will make you look like a rock star.

PRO TIP #2: If you use Draft2Digital's formatting tool, you can actually update your front and back matter in your account and tell it to ripple out to *all* your books. It's magical.

PRO TIP #3: If you use Vellum to format your books, you can make the adjustments in one Vellum file and then copy those sections or chapters into your other books for anything that is identical through every book in your series. This will eliminate the likelihood of making copy/paste mistakes. (It happens. Ahem.)

Changing eBooks

With eBooks, your changes will usually be live in 24 hours. At the time of writing, most platforms do not charge for changes to eBook text. Check your agreements with your distributor though—some do. And keep in mind if you are making very big changes to the content, you need to resubmit your files to Kindle in a particular way and request that they notify people who have purchased your book that there is an updated version available for download. This does not happen automatically. And Amazon generally will not do this for small changes or fixing typos. It has to be a change that *significantly* improves the reading experience.

The good news? As soon as the new file is published, anyone *new* who purchases the book will automatically get the most current version.

· · ·

PRO TIP: If your books are in audio format as well, changes to the text that are not made to the audio can cause Whispersync to stop working properly. If you have books in both formats you may want to wait to make your eBook changes until you can update the audiobooks, too.

Changing print books

With print on demand, it's relatively quick and easy to make changes to print books. KDP Print will not charge you to make changes. IngramSpark will. Make sure you're batching changes if you're using a service where you have to pay for changes. In fact, if you want to update your front and back matter each time you add a new book to your series, make sure you factor that cost into your budget and sustainability plan.

And remember, if the changes you are making change the page count you'll need to upload a new cover file since spine widths are determined by page counts.

PRO TIP: At the time of writing, if you're a member of the Alliance of Independent Authors (ALLi) you may be able to access a coupon code that gets you free changes to your IngramSpark files. Other writers' organizations may have similar offers available. If you have several books to update, or do updates often, it may be more cost effective to become a member of ALLi than it would be to pay for changes on each of your books each time you add a new one.

Changing audio

This is a bit more challenging (read *expensive*). Obviously for things like typos, you're not going to have to re-record the audio. But for content changes that ripple out in other places (I once realized I used the wrong name for a minor character, who becomes a main character in a future book) then you do need to correct that. Fortunately, I caught that error when I was reviewing the sample narrator files. But if you don't catch errors before you record the audio, then you have to try and get the same narrator back into the studio, correct the issue, likely pay them an hour at minimum for their time, and then republish your audiobook.

Fortunately, you are going to be strategic on the production side, so you'll have caught all the problems before the books are recorded. But, if something does slip by, because you have a handy tracking file, you're going to batch your changes so you can do all your "pickups" at the same time without worrying about anything getting lost or dropped along the way. Ideally when you've got that same voice actor in the studio recording your next book.

If you do have to make audiobook changes and don't have a next book scheduled, ask yourself if there's anything else you can get the narrator to record for you during that hour.

- Book blurbs?
- The voiceover for your book trailer?
- A call to action to add to the back of your audiobook sending people to your author website?

- An excerpt from one of your upcoming titles in the series to use as a teaser?
- Answers to some questions from your readers that you can use on your website as special promo content?

No matter what company you're using, make sure you review their guidelines for submitting changes to your audio files. And when you change things like book descriptions, it can take anywhere from a few days to a few weeks for that change to ripple out into all the distribution channels.

PRO TIP #1: If you're using Findaway Voices for distribution, at the time of writing you can only push out changes to your audiobook's metadata once a month. So make sure that you've got all your changes made before you hit that submit button.

PRO TIP #2: If you're using ACX for distribution, you'll want to follow their guidelines for changes. And you *may* need to contact support to make changes to an audiobook's info if it's already published.

Your Turn: for previously published authors

- Do you have any updates waiting to be done on your books?
- In which formats?
- Is your system for updates set up in a way that is working for you?
- Make any adjustments that are on your lists, and test out your new tracking system to make sure it's working for you.

40

LAUNCH STRATEGIES FOR SERIES

How to launch your books is a topic others have written entire books about.

There are as many different ways to do it as there are authors and series. And unfortunately this is yet another one of those areas where no one can tell you the *right* way to do it.

You'll need to look at what you want to achieve with your series (and the current book launching in it), your budget, your preferences and skills, your timeline, your stats from past launches, and then decide what components or strategies you want to use this time.

First, let's break down a few of the components of a launch and decisions you'll need to make.

Wide or exclusive?

Are you going to go exclusive to Amazon or publish wide on all the channels? Or go wide for a few months, and then go exclusive (or vice versa)? KDP Select/Kindle Unlimited requires 90 day commitments, so you *can* be exclusive and publish wide—just not at the same time!

Are you in it for the algorithms?

On many platforms, sales are sales; it doesn't matter who is buying your books, as long as someone is. On Amazon, things are a little trickier and you will want to be strategic in how you roll out your launch promo to make sure you're training Amazon's algorithms properly on who *your readers* are. Because once you've helped the bots identify who will buy your book, they know who to tell about it. And they will… because their job is selling more books. I'm not going to go into great detail here about this technical side of things—because a couple other people have done a fabulous job in explaining all of it.

Before you plan your launch strategy, I highly recommend you read the following books:

- *Amazon Decoded* by David Gaughran
- *Launch to Market* by Chris Fox

Pre-order? Yes, no, and timing

For eBooks, you can set up pre-orders a year in advance through KDP, as well as most other retailers. Yay! Right?!? Well, sort of.

Many established authors set up advance pre-orders on every channel *except* Amazon. Because those other platforms count your pre-order sales as part of your launch day numbers. But Amazon counts them as sales on the day they were made which means you're cannibalizing your rank on launch day by having your fans pre-order.

The other sticky bit is that Amazon calculates your author ranks based on how your books are selling. And that includes pre-order books (which generally don't sell as well as books people can one click and start reading right in the moment). So it can actually hurt your author rank and your ad effectiveness if you have a book up on Amazon for pre-order. That's why you'll see lots of folks doing a "soft launch" of their eBook instead of a pre-order.

What's a "soft launch"?

A "soft launch" is when you make your book live, but you don't advertise it or draw any attention to it for a little while after it's published. Often authors will do this so that their Advance Reader Copy (ARC) teams can begin posting their reviews, you can get your editorial reviews up, and if you are a new author you can claim all your author profiles in various places like Goodreads and BookBub and the various Amazon sites (US, France, Japan, Germany, UK).

Strategic series authors will quietly publish their new book, grab all their sales page links so they can set up their Universal Book Links, and then add the UBL links to their older book files and quickly republish those series titles before they start spreading the word about their new book.

Simultaneous release and launch of multiple formats of a single title

If you want to do a simultaneous release of multiple formats, you need to plan ahead. At the time of writing, there's no way to know for sure how long audio will take to become available. You can set a live date, but it's a wee bit hit or miss (in my experience) of whether or not some retailers honour that. And since audio takes so long to produce, if you want to release your audiobooks with your eBooks and print versions, you'll likely have to hold back with the book publishing.

And then distribution on audio can be three weeks or longer before it shows up everywhere once your files are ready, instead of the 12-72 hours it takes for eBooks, and the roughly two weeks it takes for print (assuming you're ordering a proof copy first before you hit the publish button).

Why do this? If it's so complicated, why would someone do this? Well, the more formats of a title you have, the more likely you are that any reader who is interested in your story will find a good fit for their preferred format. If you're looking for maximum visibility out of the gate, and you're looking to make your paid advertising work as hard as it possibly can for you, then every format you add increases your chances of converting interest to a purchase.

Are you trying to hit the top of your category?

One of the goals people have at launch is to try and hit the top of their category—or at least get into the top ten, or even top 100 as all of those will get you increased visibility on the sales platforms. If this is a goal for you, make sure you know exactly which categories you're trying to place in, and have a rough idea of how many sales are required to hit that goal. You will need to tailor your launch marketing plans accordingly. A tool like Dave Chesson's Publisher Rocket could help you figure this out.

Why do you need to know? If you're in a smaller category, you may be able to hit those top spots with just a handful of sales a day. But if your book is in a very mainstream category that you're trying to rank in (Thrillers, for example) you're going to have to sell a heck of a lot more books every day to compete with the giants in that category.

How to schedule the release of the first few books in series for maximum impact

One of the big questions authors struggle with is what the most effective way to roll out the first three books in a series.

If your stories have cliffhanger endings and you are a new author, you really don't want to keep people waiting for too long. When you don't complete the story arc in your first book, that's a great way to loop readers into your world for books two and three. But only if they don't get too frustrated with the waiting in between. Sometimes (she says from experience) a cliffhanger ending where readers can't just grab the next book will hurt you in your reviews and your readers may never come back for the rest of your books.

In fact, you might do better to release your books quite quickly, one after the other, if you have them all done and you've left people hanging. As quickly as one book every four weeks until you have the first three out. Then focus your efforts into getting new readers into book one and promoting your completed trilogy. Most authors will find that with a series, your sales really don't start to pick up until book three to five. And if it's a trilogy, lots of readers like to be able to get the whole thing and read through it at once.

If the stories are short (short stories, short reads, novellas), then you may also want to roll them out with less time between them. Assuming you can keep your momentum going by adding new things after the initial batch is released. Your goal is a regular publication schedule. So set a pattern you can stick with after you initial ones are launched.

The best release schedule to add new titles to your series to keep the momentum going

One of the stats I've read (which I can say has absolutely been backed up by watching my own sales data, but can't speak to the market as a whole) is that with each new release in a series you get a nice spike in sales of that book during release month and a boost to your read-through sales for about six weeks after launch. After that, you lose about 30% of your sales volume each month that follows without a new release.

You can keep the momentum going and more stable income between releases by:

- Using paid ads to keep driving new readers towards book one (or the first paid book in the series if book one is permafree).
- Using paid and free promotions to drive traffic into your series.
- Releasing your additional formats so that you have a new product each month or two.
- Keeping in constant contact with your mailing list (which can be easier when you have price promos to feature, and/or new formats to share with them).

The longer between releases, the more support and effort you'll likely need to put into keeping your sales stable.

What are some example launch strategies?

What I *can* do for you, is attempt to summarize some of the more popular strategies and approaches in the case studies that follow—so that you can decide what you'd like to test as part of your own process.

Keep in mind that your launch process, tools and budgets will likely evolve with every book you release. With each launch, you'll analyse what worked and what didn't and adjusting accordingly.

CASE STUDY #1: Amazon exclusive, mid-career author—CJ Hunt

Book length: novellas

Type of series: interlinked, not necessarily linear

First book in mini-series: free

New release: monthly in fall leading up to holidays, variable rest of the year

This is the process I used when I launched the last half dozen *Rivers End Romance* novellas. This works most effectively when I am releasing one new story per month— and the absolute quickest increase in momentum comes when I'm releasing a story every two to four weeks in the three months leading up to Christmas (because of my holiday romance novellas).

- Soft launch new book in series (make it available, but shhhh, don't tell anyone yet).
- Make it $0.99 and tell my Review Crew so they can get it cheap if they want to have verified reviews (I want the reviews to be verified purchases).
- Get my Review Crew to post their reviews.
- Add the book to all the places my series is listed and "claim it" on all my profiles (Amazon, Goodreads, BookBub, etc.) so that they send out new release announcements.
- Notify my list of my new release at the discounted

price to generate some momentum and secure the Also Bought algorithms.

- Wait until at least 100 sales and enough time has passed for my list to grab their copies at the discounted price—then change to regular price.
- Schedule stacked ads / promos to drive traffic to the free, first-in-series and hope that they'll "read through" all the way to the new title.
- Before promos run, email my list and ask anyone who bought the book at the discounted price to post reviews, if they are willing (which also acts as a reminder to purchase for folks who missed earlier emails).
- Release print and audiobook formats in the two months following the eBook release so I have new release product each month.
- Once I have a decent number of reviews and star ratings, start ads on the first paid book in series to support my new title and keep the sales going.
- Occasional promo blasts for the free first-in-series to keep new traffic coming to the series.
- Once the last book in the mini-series has been released, then box everything up after the first permafree book and change the call to action at the end of the first-in-series to encourage people to "complete their collection" with the boxed set.
- Set up ads on the boxed set, to keep sales consistent.
- Make notes on what worked, what didn't work and what I want to change for the next launch.
- Take a break and celebrate, then regroup, before doing it all again with the next book!

CASE STUDY #2: Wide launch, established author— Cora Seaton

Book length: full-length novels (50,000 to 80,000 words)

Type of series: interlinked

First book in series: free

New release: every 3 to 4 months

- When Cora has her series covers, and maybe a blurb for book one, she puts them on her website.
- Once the new book is there on her site, she starts letting people know it's coming with social media posts and by putting the link to pre-order the new title in the backmatter of previous books.
- She has a newsletter list just for signing up to hear about when the pre-order goes up. Depending on how far apart the books are coming out, she tries to have a pre-order up for the next book before the previous one goes live.
- Cora's pre-orders are at full price and she keeps the books at full price until book one has been up for about six months and she is ready to launch book three. Then she makes book one free and does a BookBub feature on it just before/after book three goes live.
- She gets ARC (advance reader) copies out to about 30 readers a week in advance and then prompts them to review on release day. Cora doesn't worry about verified sales, she just sends them ARC copies.

- She claims her book in various places, and
- Because she's wide (and other non-Amazon platforms are more driven by humans!) Cora also notifies the vendors a couple of months before her next release and they usually add the books to her series page and so on, so by the time she goes to claim the book it's generally linked up already. Her assistant checks on GoodReads.
- She has a large mailing list, so she breaks it into two and sends a new release email to group one on release day, to group two the next day, a reminder email to group one the third day, to group two the fourth day and then a text-only message on day five to everyone thanking them for the great release week and including some reviews and so on.
- She usually uses the BookBub new release announcement and sometimes tries for a feature announcement as well.
- She posts all over social media several times and she comments on/shares all the Tuesday release announcements from other authors that she comes across on social media.
- If she can, Cora tries to pair a new release in a series with a free deal/BookBub feature deal on book one of the series. That only works sometimes. Other times she just uses stacked ads to promote book one.

A caution about depending on BookBub feature deals

If your launch strategy includes a BookBub feature deal then #1) have a backup plan, because there's no guarantee you'll get one and #2) you'll need to space your releases out more if you're hoping for a BookBub feature on a free first-in-series or discounted first-in-series as part of your strategy for every new release—you can only feature the same book every six months. And that's only if you're chosen!

In the case above, it works because the author has multiple series on the go and can spread the releases out as needed to give space enough to potentially qualify for a BookBub feature each time.

If you are going after a feature deal, make sure you *really* familiarize yourself with BookBub's guidelines. They have shared several articles on their blog about how to improve your chances of being selected, and the specific limitations they have on what books qualify.

Key components of a successful launch

- **A mailing list**—exact numbers of people on your list will vary depending on your genre, and what stage you're at in your career. But a good goal is to be able to sell at least the first 100 books to readers on your mailing list. This will set you up with strong, relevant Also Boughts, and kick start your sales numbers. A 10% response rate of folks on your list who click to buy the book from a link you send would be quite high. Most common wisdom says to plan for about 1%. After you've had your list through a couple of launches you'll know your own stats as far as your engagement levels. If you want to be able to sell 100 books on launch day from your list, you'll likely need a list of at least 1,000 and up to 10,000 readers. *Newsletter Ninja* by Tammi Lebreque is the must-read reference book if you're not sure how to build and grow your email list.

- **An ARC Team/Review Crew**—To get that sales momentum going you really need to get a number of reviews posted right away when your book goes live. This is where your ARC Team is invaluable. *Strangers to Superfans* by David Gaughran is a great book to help you out if you're struggling with building superfans and your reader relationships. If you're new on the scene, you may need to tap into an existing ARC team using a service like Hidden Gems or BookSprout.

- **Paid Promos/Newsletter Swaps**—You need to leverage other people's lists, not just your own. These should be carefully matched genre-wise so you're attracting the *right* readers (remember the algorithms!). These work great with a free first-in-series.

- **Paid Ads**—Ads on first paid book in the series will help drive new readers into the series post-launch and keep momentum. You generally want to ensure you're making your money back on your ads, so you don't usually run ads on a free first-in-series.

Crap. I did it all wrong. Do-over?

In short, *Yes!* You can have a do-over. If you've already launched one or several books in your series, and you now realize you've done it all wrong and want to relaunch your series using all the interesting stuff you've learned in the interim, you may want to check out Chris Fox's book *Relaunch Your Novel*. It'll help you analyse what to change (and what not to change) and how to approach it to level up.

Series author JP McLean has generously shared her relaunch strategy following one such rebranding adventure.

CASE STUDY #3: Wide, rebrand and re-release—JP McLean

Book length: full-length novels

Type of series: linear

First book in series: regular price

Re-release + new release: followed the process below, after coming to the conclusion that the original covers were not accurately representing the genre of the series.

- First book in series is discounted, but not free. It sells for $2.99 USD vs $5.99 USD for the others in the series.
- Following the rebranding of the series, all the books were launched at two-week intervals.
- The first four books were re-releases and launched for a limited time (three weeks) at $0.99. During

the $0.99 sale period, the author promoted it on social media, in her newsletter and blog, and with guest blog posts. She did no paid advertising.

- The schedule of staggered launches and price increases provided a weekly announcement opportunity for either a "new release" or "get it before the price increases" notice. The two new releases were launched at their regular price of $5.99.
- Momentum built throughout the launch, fuelled by the "sale" pricing and the good fortune to also have had the first book's cover win a Kobo cover contest.

Lessons learned: Get large, solid ARC teams in place prior to launch. Reviews are critical for promotion and sales. Covers and titles more accurately in line with audience has improved sales.

Why paid first book in series? It can help read-through when you know that your readers are willing to pay for a book right from book one. Getting them to download that first book might be a bit more challenging, but once they do you're more likely to have them keep going! Unfortunately, lots of people who download free books never actually read them. And many will only continue the series if they can get the subsequent books for free as well.

PART V

SCALE UP YOUR SALES

41

EVALUATE SALES DATA

You need an accurate picture of where your sales are at before you start your promotional activities. Otherwise, how will you know whether or not your efforts are having an actual impact on sales?

How will you measure cost vs benefit if you don't keep track of how an advertising campaign or series of promotions or the release of a new title has impacted sales on all your other books?

Correct. You won't. And instead of throwing spaghetti noodles at the wall to see what sticks, you'll be throwing money. And since that money will be landing on someone else's floor, if it doesn't stick you'll be really sad. And you won't want to keep throwing money at the same wall, in the same way. You're smarter than that.

You are a strategic series author. You are going to keep an eye on your data.

There are some tools that exist specifically to help authors manage their writing and publishing businesses and to keep a handle on things like this.

Each distributor you use probably has a reporting tool of some kind on their dashboards. These vary greatly in quality of information and ease of understanding and comparison.

Many authors find using an external tool to pull all that data into one place is very useful.

KDP Dashboard has just had a pretty big overhaul, and they're testing the new Beta version now. It's much better than it was, but still doesn't bring all your products in all their formats together and it doesn't show you all your sales since the beginning of time. Just the more current info in your account.

Bookreport (https://www.getbookreport.com/) is a Google Chrome add-on that transforms your KDP Dashboard into something prettier and easier to understand. It's free until you're making more than $1000/month and then there are fees.

The challenge? Neither of these let you bring in your royalties from all the platforms and formats of your books.

ReaderLinks (https://readerlinks.com/) is one that I have been using for a couple of years and in my humble opinion it's currently the best. It incorporates sales and expense analytics, a calendar tool, book information/metadata and even has options to help you manage ARC teams all built in. It is a paid tool, with a monthly or annual fee.

And there is the option to import some platform data in a mostly automated way, and then manually add what is missing. This one also lets you enter your expenses from various promotions, add them to your tracking calendar, and then it will analyse your book sales to give you a rough ROI (return on investment) percentage for those promos so you can see what worked and what didn't.

I also love that its creators are authors themselves. And really nice people. And constantly improving the tool and adding new features. I don't know about you, but I'm happy to pay nice people who create cool and helpful things to make my life easier, so they can keep on doing it.

And the way the data is displayed inside this tool, and the way that I can analyse the different trends in my sales has been very, very influential in terms of business decisions I've made about what books or mini-series to focus on next, which markets to advertise in, and whether or not certain promotions were worth running again.

PRO TIP: If you've got a helper, you can get an admin account access set up so that your assistant can help with managing your account. Just be aware that at the time of writing, this gives them full access to everything—all dashboard data, revenue numbers and settings—in your account.

Or just make up your own tool

Like many of the other aspects of writing and publishing your series, it doesn't so much matter how you're doing it, it mostly matters that you *are* doing it. So if entering all your data on an Excel or Pages or Google spreadsheet every month is what brings you joy, then skip the tools and rock on with your badass, data-entering self.

42

GET MORE REVIEWS

Why reviews matter

In the context of scaling up sales of your books and overall on your series, reviews play a critical role. Multiple roles, really. Especially if you are early on in your series career, reviews might be the best way to scale up your sales at the beginning. Why?

- Reviews help new readers find you. Many won't take a chance on books that don't have 10+ reviews, or even 100+ in some genres!
- A certain number of reviews are required for many promo sites. The exact amounts vary from 10-100 and often these require a 4-star rating or higher.
- Reviews make your ads work better. (100 reviews on Amazon.com seemed to help jumpstart my ads. And I've heard that number from other folks, as well.)

- Reviews can trigger additional promotions from the distributors on your behalf. No one *really* knows what's going on behind the scenes, but the more good reviews you have, the more likely people are to buy your books when they are recommended to readers.

How to get more reviews

Write a good book. And then ask for reviews. Yeah, I know —crazy simple. But basically that's what it boils down to. Before you do anything though, make sure you understand the rules of reviews for the platforms you're on.

- Make sure you ask your readers at the end of the book to review if they liked it and want to help other people find your books.
- Make a review request part of your newsletter mailing list on-boarding sequence—especially if they're on your mailing list as the result of receiving a free book from you.
- Ask your readers (via your list or Facebook group or wherever) to help you reach specific goals when you've got something coming up. For example, if you know you're going to apply for a BookBub feature on your first book at a super discounted price to help launch your new book, you can let your readers know that you need their help. You could let your list download the title for free in exchange for an honest review. You can nudge everyone who has read the book and not yet left a

review to pretty please do it by x date. Thank them in advance and let them know how much you appreciate it.

Services that can help connect you to potential reviewers

You should *never, ever* use services where you pay for reviews. But… there are legit services that will connect you with their communities and then you can provide review copies to their readers who will then hopefully leave reviews for you. Do you see the distinction?

A couple of these services are:

- Booksprout
- Hidden Gems Books

Sometimes, it may make sense to invest in one of these services to get connected to people who you know are interested in reviewing. Especially at the start, before you've built your own review crew.

PRO TIP: Hidden Gems Books review spots book up quite far in advance. Some genres can be as much as a year. But because a lot of people are booking in advance and some aren't ready when their review date comes up, those times are given to other authors on the schedule. So it makes sense to book your review spot, upload your info and cross your fingers.

Building your own review crew

Often in the biz, these are called ARC teams. Some people call it a street team. I call my group the Rivers End Review Crew. All these terms are similar, and can be used fairly interchangeably as long as you know what the team is for, and you are clearly communicating that to the people who join you.

Usually you will recruit readers to be on this team organically, as you interact with folks through your mailing list or your other social channels. You send them advance copies of your books and then ask them to post reviews once your book is live.

Much like getting reviews, you have to invite people to join you on your team. The best way I've found to do this is via my mailing list. Others have great success using Facebook groups, as that's often where writers' most devoted fans hang out.

Different authors manage these groups/teams in different ways, so you will need to identify:

- What do you want your team to help with?
- What will you call them?
- How, when and where will you invite people to join your team?
- How will you reward them? (Early access to ARC copies? Special giveaways only for your team?)

Remember to review the guidelines of your publishing platform so you're not violating any terms of service with the ways you're interacting with your crew.

Especially as a series author, building strong relationships with your team will help each launch to be steadily more successful than the last. In my opinion, this is well worth the time and energy to build.

And it's also likely to save you money. Having the ability to quickly get a large number of reviews posted on any new book is going to help your ads to work, your sales to grow faster and will open up additional promotional opportunities.

You will need a way to ensure that your ARC readers can actually post on the platforms you need reviews on. Some authors have people fill out a Google Form "application" to join their team. You can ask which platforms they can review on (some folks can't post Amazon reviews if they only ever get free books and haven't spent the required $50 in their Amazon account).

If you're using a service like BookSprout to help manage your ARC team you can select which platforms are required to have a review for people to receive an ARC copy of your book.

For myself, when people ask to be part of my Rivers End Review Crew I ask them which platforms they can leave reviews on, why they want to be on my ARC team, and then I also ask them to send me one review they have left about one of my books in the past. It sounds odd, but sometimes people will ask to be on your ARC team who don't necessarily like your books. Screening your ARC readers and getting to know them better will help develop your relationships, and having the criteria that they have to leave one review on a book of yours before they join will filter out the folks who just want free books but won't actually post reviews.

To ponder: I know from talking to my Review Crew that lots of people join ARC teams because they can't afford to purchase books, or don't have a credit card. If you have a permafree book, you can direct people to that to leave a sample review. If you don't, you may want to consider making an exception if the reader says they can't afford to purchase your book and provide them with one of your older books for that test review.

PRO TIP #1: Don't send out your new release announcements to your whole list until after you've asked your Review Crew/ARC team to post their reviews. The boost in social proof will help encourage even more of the other readers on your list to purchase your latest book, and will give you a pool of reviews to pull quotes from for your announcement email.

PRO TIP #2: If you want more *verified* reviews on a title on Amazon, consider having a *really* discounted price or even setting the book to free for a day (if you're in KDP Select you can do this easily) and then only tell your VIP folks to grab their copy so their reviews are verified. Then put the book back to regular price.

Amazon's series page

Amazon has a series page function that will list all the books in your series together as a group on its own page, if the books are numbered and the series name is exactly the same in every book.

Advantages

- Having your whole series grouped together can make it easier for people to find all the books that go together.
- Amazon will often notify people who have bought one book in a series when a new one is available.
- People can buy the whole series with one click as a "bundle."

Disadvantages

- This is primarily intended for numbered series that should be read in a certain order.
- You have to get separate reviews for the series page in addition to the reviews on the individual books.
- If *any* of the books in the series become unavailable, the series bundle option disappears.
- Some lengths of stories don't qualify, so if this is part of your plan, make sure you check the guidelines page.
- You can't include "in between" numbers like 2.5, and also can't include #0—so make sure you plan carefully with your numbering and your release

order. (Note: this may have changed by the time you're reading this! Double check before you commit to your numbering structure.)

Where to focus review efforts for maximum ROI (return on investment)

Of course, in the perfect world you would give all your books equal time and attention and you would get hundreds of reviews on all of them.

However, we have limited time, resources and readers to call on for favours. And especially earlier on in your series writing career, you may be forced to choose which books to prioritize.

You always want to make sure that your first-in-series makes a great showing. Priority number one. Then, titles you are running ads or promotions on need to have a solid number of reviews with good star ratings.

43

PLAN PROMOTIONAL ACTIVITIES

First—What *is* promotion? It's all the stuff you do to grow your author platform, build your reader community, and ideally also sell your books.

How is this different from advertising? Well, it's probably not an industry-wide distinction but I find it helpful to think of advertising as stuff you pay for that leads directly to sales, and promotion as activities you may or may not pay for, but that have a goal of connecting with readers or building your platform, but does not necessarily translate *directly* to sales.

And marketing is the big umbrella term that I feel encompasses both the promotion and advertising. Basically, everything you do to connect your books to your readers.

What are you trying to accomplish with your marketing activities?

Much like your writing and publishing career in general, you need to know what you're trying to accomplish with your marketing in order to decide on an effective strategy for levelling up sales of your series.

1. Build your mailing list and followers on specific social media platforms

Gurus write long lists of all the different ways you could approach this, but for a series author the following are tried and true methods to connect and engage with readers.

- Engage in list-builder promotions with other authors using BookFunnel, StoryOrigin, Prolific Works (formerly Instafreebie), and/or BookSweeps.
- Use a "cookie" (aka lead magnet) made from a delicious short story, novella or deleted scenes from your book and give it away exclusively to people who join your list.
- Set-up giveaways and contests with a call to action like, "Follow me on BookBub/join my mailing list and be entered in a draw to win a free book."

2. Increase purchases from your existing series readers

Methods that have proven effective for series writers include:

- Asking people in your author or series Facebook group to buy a specific book.
- Asking people on your mailing list to buy your new release. This is not the same as "letting them know," you need to say, "Buy the next book in the series."
- Offering price breaks for people on your email list and/or in your Facebook group.
- Sharing excerpts and teasers from your new title that contain a "Buy now" prompt and link directly to Universal Book Link sales page.

3. Drive new readers to your series

This requires that you reach beyond your email list and the reader group you already have.

- Participate in newsletter swaps with other authors in your genre, to connect with their readers. This is most effective around a price-break promotion or new release.
- Pay to be featured on one of the big industry newsletter lists, like BookBub.
- Pay for ads on platforms where readers hang out like Amazon and BookBub, or where you can isolate readers such as through Facebook ads.

4. Improve rank and visibility for your series

- This strategy is basically using all the approaches described in **Drive new readers to your series** at once over a compressed period of time to drive your sales in an upward direction.

5. Increase KU page reads

- Share promo images that include "free to read on KU" with all your social media channels and email subscribers.
- Pay for ads that feature a short excerpt from your book. Include "Read for Free on KU" with a link to your book sales page.
- Nudge your mailing list to remind them that if they have Kindle Unlimited, they can read your book for free.
- Sign-up for a BookFunnel promo specifically to promote "read for free on KU."

6. "Hit a list"

Generally, this refers to going all in on your promotional efforts to try to get on a list like the *USA Today* bestseller list. This is risky, potentially quite expensive, and I know a few authors who have taken a run at it and been devastated when it didn't pan out. If this is the holy grail for you, all I'll say here is:

- Know what the tracking period is (i.e. to the minute when the clock starts on counting sales towards your weekly total and when it stops).
- Make sure you have wide distribution.
- Do your homework on how bestselling status is

calculated, when your best time of year is (least competition), and know the rules of the game.

- Don't invest any money you can't afford to "lose" (or feel like you lost) if you miss the list.

What kind of marketing activities are there?

Following are the different types of advertising and promotion that most series authors make use of and when. Most of these options are available to both traditionally and indie published authors, but I indicate where there might be issues or limitations for traditionally published authors.

Each of these methods have upsides and downsides, as well as being differentially effective at different stages of your book's life, and for different genres. I'm not going to tell you which are the best (there's no one right answer to this question). What I'm sharing is a quick list of the options and the different ways to strategically combine them.

Claim your author profiles

Claim every one of these profiles, even if you don't think you'll ever use it. The more places your author name appears, the better. And some places, like Goodreads, will fill up with information about your books from readers who are putting them on their 'To Be Read' or other virtual bookshelves.

· · ·

1. Social media channels

Without listing all the social media channels, the ones that many authors find valuable are Facebook, Instagram and Pinterest. Claim these as soon you can. If your author name has already been claimed by a non-author-type (the nerve!)—or a different author (even nervier!)—figure a work-around.

There was already another author named CJ Hunt when I went to claim my space on the internet. He writes non-fiction so, to distinguish myself from him I claimed CJHuntRomance for all my social media profiles (and my website URL).

If you were paying attention you might have noticed that the author name on this very book is Crystal Hunt. I am using a different author name for my non-fiction books so as not to confuse or upset my romance fans. Of course, the name Crystal Hunt is already owned. This other Crystal is not an author, she's an actress, so the way I distinguish myself from her is to be CrystalHuntAuthor on social media and, of course, on my non-fiction author website.

2. Amazon Author Central

Your Amazon.com profile is another one you absolutely must claim. Readers will look for you there, and anyone who follows you will get notifications of new releases, and you can link videos and blog posts—not to mention if they click on your author name on any of your book listings they will see *all* your books and all the formats they are available in. Don't lose a sale by making it harder than necessary to find you.

Amazon author accounts are also available on their four international sites: Japan (Amazon.co.jp), France (Amazon.fr), UK (Amazon.co.uk) and Germany (Amazon.de). Many other countries will populate your Author Page automatically by pulling the data from the Amazon.com site (alas, not Canada). There is no cost to claim your author space on these sites. You might be surprised at how many readers there are of English books in countries around the world.

Use Google Translate to help you through the sign-up process if you don't happen to speak all those languages.

3. Goodreads

On Goodreads you can claim your author profile as soon as you have your ISBN assigned to your book title or your book available for pre-order on Amazon.com since that will give you their ISBN equivalent, an ASIN. That is the number you need to enter in Goodreads to show you're an author by connecting yourself to a book. Usually each new book will automatically populate the Goodreads database (Goodreads is owned by Amazon) but you can always add it manually if your author profile is claimed and your book isn't yet showing up.

4. BookBub

Your BookBub author profile can also be claimed as soon as you have a book available for pre-order. If the title doesn't automatically show up in the BB database, send a help request and the fine folks at BookBub will manually add you.

If you are not an American author, be sure to contact support and request a US account as not all countries have the same features unlocked. You will want to be able to make book recommendations to your followers, and this is currently only available in the US accounts.

Even if you never plan to buy a BookBub ad for your books, this is well worth the 10-minute set-up time since they have free promotional services to help authors spread the word about new releases.

Before you publish

- Connect with your mailing list.
- Build buzz on social media (Cover reveals work great).
- Build your Advance Reader Copy (ARC) team.

At launch

- Encourage reviews from your ARC readers.
- Engage in newsletter swaps with authors who write in your genre.
- Set a discounted launch week or launch month price.

- Start your paid ads (after you have at least ten good reviews).

Maintain and scale-up sales

- Offer temporary price discounts for holidays or even every quarter if you're exclusive to Amazon —take advantage of the promo and free days they allow.
- Create a promotion that groups the earlier books in your series.
- Pay for ads to attract attention to the first book in your series or bundle several tiles into a boxed set and advertise that.

Know your why, and the action you want readers to take when setting up promotions and discounts

If you know the connections between your stories, it's much easier to decide which books will have the most impact if you offer promotional pricing or discounts. For example, let's say you have seven books in a shared story world. If you're launching a new book, where a minor character from book three is the main character in book seven, then it might be most beneficial to make book three your free or discounted book during launch week. And naturally, you'll include a call to action at the end of the story that calls people's attention to the fact that they can find out what happens to that character by grabbing the new book! Even better would be to put a sample chapter from book seven in the back of book three.

PRO TIP: The beauty of eBooks is that you can change the back matter in your books easily. If it's launch month for your new book, and you really want to push all the attention to the new title, you can update your other books so they all point in the direction of your new release.

Your Turn

- What are your goals for your promotional activities? Be specific—go back and read **Chapter 7: Clarify your purpose** if you've forgotten how to do this as a strategic series author.
- Think about what your promotional budget will be for your book (per week, per month and per year) —and choose that amount with the assumption that you will *not* make it back in book sales. Until you have specific data on that promotional activity for *your* book, nothing is guaranteed.
- Commit to an amount of time you are willing to spend on promotional activities (per day, per week or per month).
- Do your research and make a list of all the specific options other authors recommend for promoting books in your genre, and your length and price point.
- If there are limitations on each promotional activity (for example, a promotional site that only takes new releases, or that only does full length

books, or that you must apply for three months in advance) make note of any restrictions.

- Decide which promotional platforms and opportunities make the most sense for your genre, your specific goals, and your budget at this time.
- Set-up a system to document which promotional activities you do, and whether or not they were effective. Especially at the beginning, you need to try one thing at a time to be clear about the impact of that promotional activity on your sales. You need to know exactly what is working and what isn't, and adjust accordingly.

44

SCALE WITH ADVERTISING

The best part about a series when it comes to paid advertising is that you don't have to advertise *every* book in your series. In fact, if you approach this strategically, you only have to put ads on one or two of your titles.

And the ads for books in series typically have ·a much higher overall return on investment than ads on standalone books because of read-through—the glorious phenomenon of new readers buying and reading multiple books in your series.

What type of ads and on which books?

That depends a bit on how your series is set up and what your business development goals are. You'll have to do your own research and analysis because this is an area where things are constantly changing and the approach should be completely tailored to your own goals and products. The key determining factor of how you approach ads on your series will be what you're trying to *do* with your ads.

1. Ads to build your mailing list

Generally speaking, if you're running an ad to promote a free cookie to get folks onto your mailing list, your call to action will drive people to a landing page where they are added to your newsletter list and then sent a link to your site or to a BookFunnel download page where they grab the book, *then* get added to your list.

Either way, the goal here is that once they're on your list you'll be able to convert them into dedicated series readers who will buy every existing book in your catalogue and then anxiously await your next release so they can snap that up, too.

Key things to keep in mind:

- You will not be *directly* making money from this ad since you're collecting names in exchange for giving something away for free.
- You need to be very certain that your mailing list on-boarding process will convert subscribers into readers. Test it with some friends before you connect it to an ad.
- You need to know that your series has a solid read-through rate once you do convert that subscriber to a buyer, so that they won't just download your cookie, they'll want to read them

all. Which means buying the next books in the series.

- Facebook can be an effective platform for this type of ad.

2. Ads to get people to download a free first-in-series

If you are using advertising to direct people to your permafree first-in-series title, you will most likely be driving traffic directly to a single platform's sales page, or to a Universal Book Link or GeniusLink page that links to all the places where it's available to download.

Again, before you spend money on ads you need to be sure your read-through is solid.

For this type of ad, there are lots of platforms that work. But it's ideal to start with some of the lower cost promotional sites like Free Booksy, The Fussy Librarian, Bargain Booksy and Book Barbarian. Genre is important when choosing so do your research.

Once you have a solid number of reviews with a great star rating and you know your cover, sales copy and read-through rates are rock star, *then* try a BookBub ad on that freebie and hope that the targeted exposure will bring in lots of new readers.

Some authors find Facebook ads useful to drive people to their free first-in-series. These are expensive so you want to be pretty darned sure you'll be able to recoup the cost via read-through sales.

. . .

3. Ads on your paid first-in-series

This is a great way to use ads. And Amazon's AMS ads are a good fit for this. You're getting your book in front of readers on the platform they will buy on, and it's a single click from seeing the ad to the purchase or KU download.

Since your first-in-series book is a paid product, ideally you'll be able to do better than just recover your costs, you'll make some money on that first-in-series sale and, in a few days or weeks see a bump in sales for the other books in your series as readers finish the first and read-through.

4. Ads to promote discounts

Series authors also use ads to drive traffic to books that they discount when they're taking a run at a list, trying to hit the top of their Amazon category, and doing the work to find some new readers for their series.

The places to advertise are the same as I described in the free first-in-series section.

Some authors have found great success with Amazon's AMS ads. What do these authors and their books have in common?

- They have at least two regular-priced books in the series available after the one on sale in their series.
- They have a proven read-through.

- They analyse their ad data to ensure their average cost of sale (ACOS) is low enough to be worthwhile.
- They have a good number of reviews with high star-ratings.

5. Ads to diagnose problems in read-through

Another way series authors use ads is to diagnose problems with conversion and read-through.

For example:

1. I set up AMS ads on my book that I am confident are effective since I've gathered the knowledge I need to use 500 strategic keywords in the ads, have a tested tagline and a cover image that looks great as a thumbnail.
2. I analyse my stats for clicks from the ad to my book sales page.
3. I analyse my stats for purchases made from those clicks.
4. I analyse my KDP sales data and KU reads looking for trends.

If clicks are low

- Make sure the keywords are putting your ad in front of the right readers
- Take a hard look at your cover to make sure it's appealing as a thumbnail

- Review the text in the ad. Even changing one word can make a world of difference in ad clicks.

If clicks are high, but sales are low

- First thing to check is your KU page reads since those are not shown on your Amazon ads dashboard. Maybe books sales are low because the majority of readers in your genre are Kindle Unlimited subscribers.
- This is often a problem with targeting the wrong audience, who realize your book is not the kind they read only after they hit your sales page.
- This could also indicate that you need to take a hard look at your book description if it's not convincing the folks who were lured by your cover to actually click and make the purchase.
- Or, it may be your price point is too high or too low. Yeah, it's just like *Goldilocks and the Three Bears*. You need to be in that "just right" middle spot.

When to start ads?

While there's no strict rule on this, and you can start ads as soon as your book is available for pre-order, though unless you already have an established readership, this is really risky.

Ads work best when you have a good number of reviews, with at least a 4-star average. And while the exact number of reviews to warrant "a good number" is genre dependent, it seems like books with 100+ reviews generally do better converting readers than those with fewer. Once you hit that threshold, both Amazon and the readers take you more seriously.

So, from a strategic series author perspective, the "best" time to start ads is after you've done all the work needed to get those first-in-series reviews—or whichever book in your series you're planning to advertise.

When to scale up your ad spends?

It's time to scale up your ad spends when you have hard data to support that it's working, and the money is coming in from sales to back that up.

You want to make sure that you have good read-through and your reviews are stellar. Everything should be running smoothly and your product should be fully tested and reader-approved before you try to go big. Otherwise, your money won't be working as hard as it could for you.

Your Turn

- Make some notes on what specifically you want your ads to help you achieve.
- Do your research and decide which ads platforms make the most sense for your goals, your budget and your risk tolerance.
- Calculate your read-through percentages (or at least get a solid idea) for your series

- Review your conversion rates on your newsletter (how many people click on your buy links).
- Ask yourself if you're ready to start ads, or scale up ads—depending on where you're at in your career.
- Set-up a system to document your stats, your spends, your patterns and when you change something. You need to know exactly what is working and what isn't, and adjust accordingly and you can only do that with a clear data record.

Need to gather more info before your Action phase?

There are many different platforms that you can pay for advertising on (Amazon Advertising, Bookbub, Facebook and many others), and I would highly recommend you work through a Knowledge phase before you dive in on any of these platforms. There are many authors sharing the information they've gathered about using these ads platforms. You can visit The Creative Academy website for suggestions of which are the best starting places for books, resources and courses—both free and paid.

45

CREATE MARKETING MATERIALS

You've developed your plan about what kinds of ads and promotions you're going to do. Now you're going to need some creative assets to put into play.

When it comes to creating marketing materials, a lot of authors feel pretty intimidated. You see other people posting these gorgeous pictures of 3D book covers on their social media accounts. First of all, stop comparing! Aspire, certainly, but don't despair that you're not at that level *yet*.

If you're paying for a cover design, find out if your designer offers an upgrade option to create marketing images. It may not be a lot more to have a dozen or so images created for promotions and ads. And since you know what your options are (from reading the last two chapters), you should be able to pull together a list of the images that you will likely need.

If adding more money to design is outside of your budget I've got you covered with loads of great DIY options that don't require knowing how to use Photoshop.

Whether you are indie published or traditionally published, there are several stellar tools that require very little technical or design knowledge to help you rock the marketing images for your series. And the only visual asset you need to get started is your book cover image.

But first things first. Before you can dive into creating images to blast out into the world, you need to hammer down a few branding details because consistency is key if you're going to portray yourself as a pro in the market place. These apply whether you're hiring a professional or doing the design work yourself.

If branding isn't something you've really given much thought to, you might want to work through the six short **Build Your Author Brand** modules you can access at creativeacademyforwriters.com/resources/strategic-seriesauthor. I'm super passionate about this and know first-hand how much of a difference solid branding can make to the success of your author career and your series.

Know your author brand

What are the elements of your author brand? You need to know where your name and your brand are positioned in the marketplace to make sure everything that is part of your series marketing enhances, reinforces and builds your overall author brand.

Your series is an extension of you as an author. The book covers don't have to have the same fonts, colours or feel as your author brand, but they should at least be *coherent*.

Know your series brand

What if you have published—or plan to publish—more than one series? The most important consideration in creating your marketing materials, which includes your cover designs, is that it should be crystal clear to readers which books belong together and which ones are not part of the series they're following (at least for now).

Know your genre

When you're creating your marketing materials, it's super important to know the conventions of your genre. For example, if you write super sweet, clean and wholesome romances and you choose images for your marketing materials that feature a half-dressed couple in a passionate lip-lock, you are very likely going to disappoint readers when they realize that the steam you promised with your cover image isn't going to be delivered in your story.

Every element of your marketing images should fit your genre. Your font choices, images, your book cover and the feel of it all together should be looked at as one piece of art.

Your Turn

- What elements of your author brand need to be present in your series marketing images? (Fonts? Colours? Logo?)
- What elements of your series brand should be present on all your marketing images? (Fonts? Colours? Logo? Character image? Series title?)
- What genre conventions or standards do you need to adhere to?
- What restrictions, if any, do the platforms you intend to share these images on have related to? (No naked torso, no weapon, no blood, etc.).

DIY options

Even if you don't have the dollars to hire a pro, with the tips above and the tools below you can create good enough for now materials that will do the job until your royalties warrant paying a professional designer.

Canva (free and $)

Canva is a great free tool that is filled with templates for different kinds of visual projects. While not created *specifically* for authors, it has book cover templates and all the social media post sizes you'll ever need. It also provides design layouts and images, some free, some for $1 per use.

• • •

allauthor (free and $)

allauthor.com has a magic tool that can help you make 3D cover images in various configurations. You can make great looking images just by uploading your covers and choosing which configuration of books you want them to appear on. There is a limited set of images you can use for free, and then you need to pay to upgrade to Pro if you want to unlock the whole image library.

Book Brush ($)

This is a fantastic tool, built specifically for non-technical authors. You upload your covers and then put them into all kinds of cool templates for images that are custom created at the proper sizes for different platforms and purposes. You can also design ads and create animated little video clips with your books. And there's a big library full of community templates to use. It's very cool. And also very affordable. About the same for a one-year license as 1-2 hours of a graphic designer's time.

Covervault.com (free) + Photoshop ($)

A graphic designer named Mark has created a ton of templates in CoverVault that work if you have Photoshop. You download the template for free, open the file and swap out your cover for the placeholder cover. You can change the background images too, and turn layers/objects on and off as you like. Et voila! Gorgeous 3D images.

He also has a Pro collection which you can purchase if you want more than what you find on the site. If you have a really long series or large boxed sets and need the templates for those, you'll find them in the "big collection" of materials.

Photoshop licenses are available for a reasonable monthly subscription fee—far less than you would pay for an hour of a graphic designer's time. If you love learning new software, bundling this with Covervault is a cost-effective way to build your marketing asset library.

License your images

No matter what tools you use to create your marketing images, it's critical that the images you use are from licensed sources. **Do not** just do a Google image search and grab the images you like without following them back to the source, and making sure you're able to use them without paying a licensing fee to the photographer or creator. If a fee is required, and that's the image you want then pay for the license, and carefully read the instructions about any requirements for crediting your source.

If you're using BookBrush, Canva or the Covervault.com templates then as a general rule any of the images they have included in those tools have been properly sourced. However, it's still up to you to do your due diligence on anything that you are adding to the mix.

If you are hiring a designer, make sure you check with them about the images they are using and how/where they are licensed from. Sometimes, you might be better off to license the images yourself, and then have the designer combine them with your text. This is especially true if you want to use the same image in multiple promotional images, or have it to work with again in the future. If you let the designer license the image, then technically they can use it in any of their projects, and you can only use it in what they give you. Check the licensing guidelines—every stock image site is a bit different in what they allow.

Where to get free and affordable stock images?

The list of free sites is always changing, so I'm not going to be specific here. But if you Google "sites for free stock photos" you'll get several articles with lists of the most current options for you.

To get affordable images from various paid stock sites, I recommend that you sign up to a variety of newsletters for different stock images sites. Often they send out free images of the week. You can start building your collection. They will also let you know when they have sales or specials running.

Black Friday is usually when many companies offer sales for either annual licenses, or a batch of stock image credits. You can stock up your supply for the rest of the year.

And some sites will give you x number of images for free, or x days of a free subscription with no commitment beyond that.

PRO TIP #1: From most stock sites, you can download a "comp" version of an image for free to use when you're drafting up layouts. Then once you've confirmed for sure which images you need in your final products, you license just the ones you need.

PRO TIP #2: When you're downloading images from any stock site, leave the original filename intact so you know how to credit it and where it came from, and just add your own identifier to the filename at the start so it's easy to see at a glance what it is. Here's an example using the filename of a photo that I licensed from DepositPhotos—including the book name of what I'll use the picture to promote (His+Hers), as well as a descriptor (BrigidsReadheadTwins), and then the Depositphotos original Title.

Renamed Title:

His+Hers_BrigidsRedheadTwins_Depositphotos_151117736_s-2019.jpg

Develop a checklist

Having a checklist of marketing images that you need each time you release a new book will streamline this end of your strategic series author business. Some common types of marketing images to create for each book in your series are:

- $0.99 sale
- $2.99 sale
- Read for Free on KU
- New release
- cover as 3D (print book)
- cover on a tablet (eBook)

- All the books in your series together
- Animated cover image clip for video promo

And you will likely want a version of each of these that is optimized for each social media platform you're on, or each place you're going to be connecting with your readers to share your posts.

Your Turn

- What tool(s) are you going to use to create your marketing images?
- What do you need in your set of marketing images for each book in your series?
- If you created a spreadsheet that contains tabs to track your timeline, places, characters and world, add a tab for your marketing assets.

PART VI

GROW YOUR CAREER

46

AVOID BURNING OUT

One thing that is extremely important when it comes to series writing is avoiding burnout. And burnout is sneaky, it can come in many forms: physical, mental, emotional and creative.

With each new book you write, publish and launch out into the world, your opportunities as well as your responsibilities will grow exponentially.

Putting some strategies in place before you reach a critical point will help ensure that you can keep on building on your series momentum for weeks, months and years to come.

Avoid physical burnout

Writing often means being stationary for long periods of time, most likely sitting at a desk typing for hours on end.

And if you're writing a series, you're likely going to be pushing towards that next book All. The. Time.

Repetitive strain injuries are common for writers. You need to make sure you're doing what you can to keep your body —your most important tool!—running well.

You need to take frequent stretch breaks, time away from the computer for your eyes, time away from the keyboard for your hands, time away from being inside for your mental health as well as the benefits that come from being active.

When it comes to writing, more time is not always better. As you become more successful and have the opportunity to write full time, you need to think about what that means for your body. And ensure that whatever patterns you're setting up are sustainable for you mentally, emotionally, and physically.

Some strategies to keep your body healthy and avoid physical burnout include:

- Using a standing or walking desk
- Using dictation software
- Setting the timer to take a stretch break for 5 minutes every half-hour
- Getting enough sleep
- Making exercise a priority

Avoid mental burnout

Mental burnout is when you are so tired that your brain just isn't working right. You make mistakes, you overlook things, you take simple answers because thinking of anything more complicated seems exhausting. The time you do spend working doesn't yield the results you're looking for.

Ways to help avoid mental burnout include:

- Ensuring you have quiet times built into your schedule for rest and relaxation
- Daily meditation
- Engaging in hobbies that let your mind rest, like knitting, colouring, playing an instrument
- Spending time in nature (Ever hear of "forest bathing?" Seriously, Google it.)

Avoid emotional burnout

Emotional burnout is when you hit a wall and you just don't feel like working on your series anymore. This may come across as self-doubt, boredom, exhaustion or frustration but the root of the problem is that you've lost your passion for your work or for this particular series.

Maybe you got a less than stellar review which has crashed your excitement around your series. Maybe you're just tired. Maybe something has happened in your life which has used up the emotional energy you normally dedicate to your writing. Maybe the topic you're writing about has dredged up emotions from your past that you need to process. The possibilities are endless.

Solutions?

- Have a support system of friends, family and other writers to talk to
- Talk to a professional (counsellor or writing mentor)
- Give yourself a break and focus on self-care for a bit
- Break out your happy file of good reviews and read through it

Avoid creative burnout

There are two different ways I personally look at creative burnout.

The first type happens when we're constantly creating, always focused on output. In those periods we may not take enough time to "refill the well."

It's tempting to hunker down and go hard toward getting your series written, but unless you're working on a series with a clear end point, there's pretty much always going to be another book to write. You need to ensure you're taking breaks and taking in inspiration, breathing fresh new life into your creativity so that you're growing alongside your story and your readers.

The other kind of creative burnout happens when the energy or passion for a project gets "used up" and we find ourselves struggling to finish something because we've promised it to our readers, but we're not all fired up about it anymore.

How can you avoid creative burnout?

- Build your series in a way that gives you flexibility around how many books need to be released.
- Set a somewhat flexible publication schedule so that you can work through creative issues that pop up.
- Have an adventure in real life that will help inspire you or "fill the well" of creativity again.

Your Turn

- Brainstorm a list of things you could do (or not do) that might help you avoid or recover from **physical burnout**. Then arrange your environment to support those behaviours.
- Choose at least one thing that will help you avoid **mental burnout** and make time for it in your daily routine or on your calendar.
- Identify three people (or groups) you could call on when you need a bit of a boost **emotionally**. Beside each name write the best way to communicate with them (in-person, phone, email, online forum, etc.).
- Make a list of things that help to **fuel your creativity**. Then schedule in some time on your calendar to regularly engage in those activities.

47

CELEBRATE YOUR WINS

When you're embarking on a long-term project like writing a series, it's more important than ever to make sure you're celebrating your wins along the way because it's possible you might never be "done." As long as you're writing, you need to identify milestones that you can easily recognize as celebration moments.

For me, finishing the first draft of any project is the hardest stage, and the step where I'm most likely to get derailed.

There's risk involved in finishing a story, because then it's time for other people to read it and weigh in on its strengths and weaknesses. This is why, for me, the milestone that I celebrate is when I hit that finished first draft.

I love the idea of actually popping the cork on a bottle of champagne whenever I complete a draft of a book… but because I write a lot of novellas, it seemed a bit excessive to drink a whole bottle of bubbly every time I finished a story.

However, I found these little mini-bottles of bubbly that hold just enough for a glass and a half in each bottle. The perfect solution!

I have my series planned with titles for a dozen more stories already figured out. Part of my motivation to push through finishing my first drafts happens every time I open my fridge door: I label those little bottles of champagne with my book titles, one bottle per title. It's a great way for me to celebrate finishing one stage of my book's life and it keeps me on track, focused on my goal.

What to celebrate

Celebrating where you're at and how far you've come is extremely important. It's easy to get swept into a constant round of doing and not look back at how far you've come.

If you were paying attention to the chapter on avoiding burnout, you know why it's important to recognize these in-between moments. If you don't already celebrate milestones, here are some ideas to consider:

- Finishing a first or final draft of a story
- Publishing the first, next, or last book in a series
- Reaching a certain number of KU downloads in a month (set several milestones—1,000, 10,000, 100,000, 1 million)
- Reaching a certain number of newsletter

subscribers (set several milestones—100, 500, 1,000, 5,000)

- Hiring a designer to create your series marketing materials
- Surviving a book launch week

How to celebrate milestones

Your celebration doesn't have to be about champagne— you can choose anything you like to celebrate. The members of our Creative Academy shared some of the ways they celebrate reaching milestones in their writing and publishing lives.

- Buy a box of fancy chocolate
- Have a spa day
- Drink bubbly water from a fancy glass
- Buy new tea and a new mug
- Go out with a friend

Turning daily habits into rewards

Sometimes, just showing up and doing the work is what we need to celebrate. But most of us don't. We simply expect that of ourselves, forgetting that this level of commitment to becoming a strategic series author is honestly, celebration-worthy every single day. In the spirit of avoiding burnout, here's a snapshot of my workday so you can see how I use my daily habits as little rewards that allow me to acknowledge that I am making progress on a big goal.

Example: Daily habits as a reward

Habit #1: Get up at 6:30am so I can be at my desk writing by 7:30am

Reward #1: Half an hour reading non-fiction, then journaling

Habit #2: Write non-fiction words for 90 minutes

Reward #2: Make myself a fancy tea latte

Habit #3: Write fiction words for two hours

Reward #3: Check my sales stats for my romance books

How to celebrate sticking with daily writing habits

Here are a few more ideas from members of The Creative Academy on how they celebrate putting butt in chair and doing their author job.

- Take a bath with a fancy bath bomb
- Take an hour to read a good book
- Buy a new book
- Spend one guilt-free hour on social media
- Watch a movie
- Engage in a weekend Netflix binge

Your Turn

- Make a list of the writerly tasks you generally complete during the course of your day.
- Make a list of the writerly tasks you'd like to be doing every day.
- Now go through your two lists and put a star beside any of the tasks you really enjoy doing, or that give you a boost when you complete them. These are your "reward tasks."
- Match your "reward tasks" with the ones that are less intrinsically motivating—the ones you're doing every day but would like to be doing.
- Brainstorm a list of some of your larger milestones for your series and your writing life, and then brainstorm ways to celebrate each of them. File that info somewhere in your shiny file system, post it on your office wall, or turn it into a bingo card of milestones you keep taped to the wall behind your monitor. Then scratch off a square each time you hit one.
- Join our "Celebrate our Success" community at creativeacademyforwriters.com and post your wins, big and small, so we can celebrate right along with you.

48

READ YOUR REVIEWS

Do you read your reviews?

Did just *reading that heading* give you a sick feeling in the pit of your stomach? Yeah, I hear ya. Reading reviews of your books is slightly terrifying. You'll hear mixed advice from people ranging from "ignore them completely" to "read every new one on a daily basis." I'm going to advocate for something in the middle. I think this can be both part of celebrating your wins, and helping you to reflect and evolve as a strategic series author.

But it does need to be handled carefully.

Why should you read your reviews?

Your reviews' most important function for you, a series author, is as a goldmine of harvestable information to help you make your next book better and your series more saleable.

For readers, it's legitimacy. No one believes that any book with 400 5-star reviews got those legitimately. Readers will assume, probably correctly, that the author was paying people for them. Having a mixed bag of reviews actually makes people more likely to trust the good ones. Your target is always for the *average* to be 4 stars or higher, as this is the threshold for many promo sites, and many readers don't read things that have less than a 4-star average.

If you're stuck in the less than 4-star ghetto, then your goal needs to be connecting with more of the right readers who will love your book (potentially after correcting the issues that the original reviewers so helpfully drew your attention to).

Even though reviews can sometimes be hard to read, it's extra important to know when your readers are not happy with something in your book or story when you're dealing with a series. The last thing you want to do is repeat mistakes that upset readers, or miss opportunities to deliver a stronger story to give those readers the extra nudge to become superfans.

Some of my most important lessons have come from my least positive reviews as they told me very specifically what the readers didn't like in my stories. This gave me the knowledge I needed to make informed decisions about my future books.

Here's a list of things I've learned from reading my reviews. These may not apply to all fiction. My series is contemporary, hometown romance:

1. Don't leave readers waiting too long for a conclusion to a story

- If your series is linear and you don't get to the conclusion of the story arc in book one, make sure the next book in the series is available so readers can get the conclusion they're looking for.
- If you write romance, make sure the HEA is clear at the end of every book, even if it's only HEA for now.

2. Readers love to hate a good villain

- They love it even more if you can turn around and make them like him down the line.

3. Don't have too many open mini-series

- I ended up writing several book ones since all my stories weave together and it was necessary in my big picture publishing plan. But in the short-term it frustrated some of my readers.

4. Don't kill off beloved characters if you don't have to

- Readers got super attached to one of my secondary characters that I originally intended to kill off in a future book. But they're all asking for her to get her own book. Of course, I'll give her her own book and kill off some other poor character instead!

5. Use the right promotional lists

- A large number of my Review Crew came from people who joined my mailing list based in large part by a promo to a list with a lot of "clean romance" readers on it. I have swearwords and sometimes even sex in my books. Those readers who want clean romance didn't like what they read and that was reflected in my reviews. Audience matching, and screening out incorrect fits, is super important to having happy readers who leave positive reviews.

When should you read your reviews?

You know yourself and what's best for you. I found that if I read reviews while I'm writing my work-in-progress, it is easy to get pulled into a spiral of self-doubt. No matter how many great reviews I get, I still focus right in on the one not so great one and spiral downwards, second-guessing everything that may have led to that review.

This is not helpful when I'm trying to get through my first draft, which I already know will fight me to the finish line.

Here's what I've found does work for me: I read my reviews when I'm in the stage between books, just as I'm getting ready to outline my next story. This is a good time to make notes of commonly recurring themes or comments in reviews since I can choose to address them in my next book or not.

How should you read your reviews?

First of all, sort them so that all your star ratings are together. That way you won't be sideswiped by a 1- or 2-star review when you're not expecting it. Also, it makes the task of finding themes a whole lot easier.

Start with your 4-star reviews and read them closely. Make a note of recurring themes. These readers enjoyed your story even if they have something critical to tell you. These reviews are gold.

Then read your 3-star reviews. Again, make a note of recurring themes. These readers may not have *loved* your story, but recognize that lots of readers never give a 5-star review, consider 4-stars excellent, and 3-stars their "good" rating. Give solid weight to these opinions.

Now it's time to tackle those annoying 1-star and 2-star reviews. Read these quickly and with purpose. Skim them. Write down keywords that jump out at you. Do not hang around obsessing. These are not your readers. Your main take-away should be to ensure your marketing does not lead people like this back to your series.

Remember that sometimes we end up with folks reading our books who were not the intended audience. This can be the result of cover issues, a mistargeted blurb or a promo to the wrong list. Sometimes the worst reviews have nothing whatsoever to do with the quality of your story or your writing. They have to do with the quality of your marketing.

Finally, you get to read your beautiful 5-star reviews. Odds are that you won't find anything in these reviews to fix in future stories, but you might learn about what your readers absolutely love (like that character you'd intended to kill off in the next book!). Write down recurring themes one more time and celebrate the fact that all those readers loved your book.

Where should you read your reviews?

1. In public or in private?

This may seem like kind of a weird question, but anyone who's ever staged a breakup with the goal of avoiding drama knows that if you do it in a public place it dampens the over-the-top emotions. If you want to keep yourself from spiralling into a jag of ugly crying if you don't like what you see, then consider checking reviews and extracting the useful info from them in a public place like a library or coffee shop.

2. On your phone, tablet or laptop?

Again, I can hear you say—does this matter? But I kind of think it does. Personally (since Scrivener rocked my world with an iOS app) I write on my phone with a portable external bluetooth keyboard. No distractions, it keeps me completely focused and the screen is so small I can't be questioning what I've written because I can barely see it. Laugh if you like, but my highest word count day to date—13,232 words—was done with that combination of tools (and a looming deadline as motivation, naturally).

Which brings me to why you might want to think about where you check reviews. My writing set-up is all about writing like the wind with a mind free from editorial commentary and self-doubt. Checking my reviews, reviewing what people didn't love about past stories? Not something I want to add into my creative space mojo.

Whereas I do sometimes write on my laptop (most often non-fiction books), most of my time on there is editing, business planning, responding to readers, outlining— things that by their very nature invite review and mental processing in a very different way.

One is art, one is business.

I write in my comfy beanbag chair on my office floor, usually in my pyjamas. I do business at my desk in my proper rolling chair and wearing grown-up clothes. Or at least real pants. These are small distinctions, but they make a big difference to me.

I love my book babies. I love my characters. And yes, my tender feelings do get hurt when people say negative things about what I have created. I suspect I'm not alone in that.

However, as strategic series authors, you and I both understand that this is business. Keeping my creative self away from the naysayers helps me to mine what I can from the reviews to hand over to my business self, and keep moving forward with my hopeful, pyjama-clad writing spirit intact.

3. On your Amazon book listing or in your Amazon Author account?

Yep. Again with the weird questions. Just like my space and technology separations, I have separations in how I interact with Amazon, too.

My book listings are like the school pictures you get of your kid. Hair brushed, shoes polished, best foot forward for the world to see. There, I'm a proud parent sharing my book babies with the world. That's where the positive editorial reviews, the star ratings, the lovely ranking in different categories shows up. This is a happy space, not meant for negative ninnies.

My Amazon Author dashboard is the place I go to do business: to see my author rank, review my books' and series' overall rankings, check that my bio links have a call to action for people to follow me and find me on my website, and post the occasional video.

There is also a handy tab for reviews where I can see *all* my reviews in one place. It also very conveniently marks any that are new since I last logged into my account.

4. Call a friend

One additional benefit of using your Amazon Author dashboard is that you can log into it separately from your publishing account. And that is particularly helpful if you really can't look at the negative reviews yourself. You can log into your dashboard and ask a friend to skim through your reviews for you while you do the same for them. A straight up laptop swap, with a couple cups of coffee (or glasses of wine—do what you gotta) and you're golden.

If you're not near your friend, you can also do this just by giving them the links of your books on Amazon and then returning the favour for them.

What should you do with the reviews?

The negative reviews

You should take notes on general trends and keywords. That's it, usually.

There are a few things you should *never* do, though. One is get into a debate with a reader or try to argue your case. It's their opinion, and you will not change it.

If you really feel you *need* to respond, write your response on a piece of paper. Then burn it. Or write an email *to yourself*, explaining the situation and then delete it. Or call a friend and commiserate. Start a monthly virtual hangout with some author friends where you compete for who got the worst review since your last meeting and then that person gets bragging rights. Or a crown. Whatever. Do whatever you have to do to shake it off, but do it privately.

Now, if a negative review includes bullying or offensive language, or the reviewer says something like, "This book sucks. You should read x,y,z book by so-and-so instead," you can do something. You hit the Report to Amazon button *and let them sort it out*. Odds are, Amazon will remove the review.

I'd originally called the next section "the good reviews" but the reality is even negative reviews can be good reviews if they give us valuable information.

The positive reviews

I covered this earlier: make notes of the themes, what people are loving in your story and what they're looking forward to with your characters.

Some people like to copy and paste their 4-star and 5-star reviews into a Word document so they have a record of them. I tend to do that for my favourites and I add them to my "happy file." That's also where I put lovely things readers have emailed to me about my books and my writing.

Then, when the Doubt Gremlins have their claws in me, I can inoculate myself with happy before diving back into the writing. I like to re-read these good reviews before starting a new book. I find it's really motivating to know that there are readers who care about my characters and my world as much as I do.

Your Turn: new series author

- Create your Happy File so it's waiting for those first good reviews to come in from beta readers and your ARC team.

- Leave a great review on a book you loved. You're going to send some of that good energy out into the writerly world so the stocks are all nicely replenished when your turn comes around. Heck, feel free to start with this book! I don't mind being the focus of your homework and this new series can use all the good juju it can get.

Your Turn: established series author

- If you don't yet have a Happy File or the equivalent, create one and paste in your best reviews, the ones that make you feel all warm and fuzzy inside and light you up with the passion to get back to that next book. Save that somewhere easily accessible for the days when the writing gets hard.
- Skim the reviews from inside your author dashboard or look through the book listing and make a list of all the keywords and things people loved and didn't love about each of your published books in the series. Each time someone else says the same thing, make a tally mark beside that keyword/phrase on your list.
- Look at all the things that have multiple mentions. Is there anything that you could do to easily fix the issues in that book? (e.g. If people are complaining about typos, can you go through your book again yourself, hire an editor, ask a friend to take a look, or use a tool like ProWritingAid to clean it up and republish?)

- Check to make sure your book is in the right genre categories and sub-categories so that they're connecting with the right readers.
- If you have an author assistant and you don't want to do this job yourself, add it to their regular task list.

49

REFLECT AND EVOLVE

With each book that you publish, you're going to get better. Why? Because you're going through this reflection and evolution process at each stage and making consistent, incremental improvements to the way you do things.

If you're a first time or new series author, focus on doing that reflection of each stage in your process, and make some notes to refer back to. Seriously, you're going to learn more in the next few months and years that come between releases than you even know exists right now. And most of the important insights and reflections you'll have about what worked or didn't work for you will *not* stay in your brain until you cycle around to this phase again.

Be kind to future you. That strategic series author is going to be killing it trying to get your series out in the world. Make their job easier any way you can.

Your Turn: new series author

- Think about where you're at in the process right now.
- What stages of writing and publishing your series have you already completed?
- Make some notes for future you about things you might tweak/do differently next time in each of the stages that you *have* completed: administration/organization, planning, writing, pitching, publishing, and promoting.

If you're already an established series author you have an opportunity to look back over your past books, your past processes and systems, and revamp those so that going forward you're bigger, badder, bolder, more organized and you're 100% ready to level-up your backlist sales and crush your next launch.

And since it's quite possible you haven't been making notes along the way about all the things you would change, let's get some of that out of your head and into your notebook or project planning software before you forget any more of the details.

Your Turn: established series author

- What worked particularly well for you at each

stage of writing, publishing and launching your last book?

- Anything you would do differently next time in each of those areas?
- Are there any areas you would like to see improvements in next time that require you to revisit the Knowledge phase?
- If yes, what do you need to research before next time?
- Where will you go to find that information?
- What specific new goals are you setting for yourself?
- How will you keep track of progress made in each of these areas after you implement those changes/know which of those changes worked?
- If you think that a fresh start is the way to breathe new life into an existing series, read Chris Fox's book, *Relaunch Your Novel*.

A note about relaunching an existing series

Sometimes, relaunching your series is absolutely what makes the most sense to create new momentum. Just think about how much you've learned along the way and how many things you'd do differently if you were starting fresh, with today's knowledge and experience.

That might feel like taking a step backwards, but remember, you're on your way to the top. It just makes sense to ensure the platform you're standing on is as solid as it can possibly be.

50

RIDE THE WAVE OF SUCCESS

Writing and publishing aren't quite as physical as surfing, but there are definitely some similarities. You paddle, and paddle, and paddle, and some days you might be the only person out there in a big, wide ocean.

Then you're at the mercy of the tides and the winds and the weather as you wait for that perfect wave, for that exhilarating ride when you're on top of the world and flying.

Those moments may be few and far between at the beginning, but you're building your pool of assets as you go. You're gaining experience. You're perfecting your balance.

And when that perfect publishing wave comes, you're going to be ready to ride it all the way onto those bestseller lists.

Success attracts success. As your series grows, your readership grows, your income grows and so does your visibility in the marketplace—and new opportunities will start to *find you*.

Some examples of these types of opportunities include:

- Being approached by companies looking to buy your book rights or license subsidiary rights
- Inclusion in special marketing programs and features with your distributor/booksellers
- Invitations to join other authors in boxed sets or big promotions
- Invitations to speak at conferences and/or attend book signing events
- Financial bonuses like KDP All Stars
- Hitting bestseller lists
- Being nominated for awards and winning contests
- Offers to turn your books into movies or TV shows
- And all kinds of things we haven't even thought of yet.

I would love to celebrate all those exciting milestones with you! And the smaller ones along the way, as well.

One of the best ways to contribute to your own success is actually by helping others ride that wave right along with you.

The final **Your Turn** exercises below will help you secure a spot in our mighty network of fantastic writers, as well as earn you some great karma points. And you just never know when those might come in handy.

Your Turn

Exercise 1: Leave a review

I hope you found this book helpful. I'd be forever grateful if you took a moment right now to post a quick review wherever you bought your copy, and on Goodreads and/or BookBub if you have accounts there.

Your review will help other writers find the book.

It also helps me know what you found most helpful. This book is part of a series and your feedback will ensure our next books give you more of what you liked–so if you include that in your reviews we'll see it and take note!

Exercise 2: Share with a friend

The only thing better than writing and reading books is sharing books with friends. If you know other writers who are interested in writing series, please let them know you enjoyed this one and found it helpful.

Exercise 3: Join our Mighty Network of Writers

Having a community who understand what you're going through as a writer makes all the difference between getting stuck or getting done. Join our **https://creativeacademyforwriters.com/join-us** and get access to a wealth of our best resources.

Exercise 4: Check out the other books in this series

It's always sad when you come to the end of a book. But the brilliant part about a series is that the fun doesn't *really* have to end! So put away your Kleenex. We've got more books in this series to help you along your writing and publishing journey. If you visit our books page at **creativeacademyforwriters.com/books** and get on our mailing list we'll let you know every time we add a new book to the series so you don't miss out!

Exercise 5: Check out the Strategic Authorpreneur Podcast

For more great info on saving time, money and energy as you level up your writing career check out the **https://strategicauthorpreneur.com/**.

More Creative Academy Guides for Writers Books

We've got a whole series of books to help you along your writing and publishing journey.

Available in eBook & print

Scrappy Rough Draft by Donna Barker
Build Better Characters by Eileen Cook
Strategic Series Author by Crystal Hunt
Create Story Conflict by Eileen Cook
Full Time Author by Eileen Cook and Crystal Hunt

Come visit us...
www.creativeacademyforwriters.com

ACKNOWLEDGMENTS

You may have noticed that this book contains a *lot* of information. It would have been a lot more confusing without the invaluable input of my two co-authors in this series—Donna Barker and Eileen Cook. You helped me carve it up, and put it back together again multiple times to ensure would make sense to more people than just myself. Thank you for all the encouragement along the way, and for seeing the book I wanted this to be.

To the other series authors at all phases of their careers who contributed suggestions and gave feedback on draft versions of this book, and generously allowed me to include information about their processes and procedures... ALL. THE. THANKS. Cora Seaton, Odette Stone, JP McLean, Michele Amitrani, Bonnie Jacoby, Alisa Luke and Natasha Pow—you're the best! So glad to have you as part of our Creative Academy family.

I'd like also to extend a thank-you to the hundreds of other authors out there who have so generously shared their learnings over the years via blogs, podcasts and resources to help people get started or level up their careers. It has made my journey a great deal easier to be able to learn from other series authors out there doing their thing.

The writing and publishing journey is always more fun with friends.

So thank you to you, dear reader, for sticking with me all the way through :) Best of luck on your **strategic** series writing and publishing journey.

RESOURCES—BOOKS

Handwritten notes:
P260
Strangers to Superfans by David Gaughran
P256
Launch to market by Chris Fox

Amazon Decoded by David Gaughran (free download from DavidGaughran.com)

✓ *Build Better Characters: The psychology of backstory & how to use it in your writing to hook readers* by Eileen Cook, The Creative Academy, 2019

Killing it on Kobo by Mark Leslie Lefebvre, Stark Publishing, 2018

Newsletter Ninja: How to Become an Author Mailing List Expert by Tammi L. Lebrecque, larks & katydids, 2018

Relaunch Your Novel: Breathe Life Into Your Backlist by Chris Fox, 2017

Romancing the Beat: Story Structure for Romance Novels by Gwen Hayes, 2016

Save the Cat! Writes a Novel by Jessica Brody, Ten Speed Press, 2018

✓ *Scrappy Rough Draft: Use science to strategically motivate yourself & finish writing your book* by Donna Barker, The Creative Academy, 2019

✓ *Start With Why* by Simon Sinek, Portfolio, 2009

The Emotional Wound Thesaurus by Angela Ackerman and Becca Puglisi, JADD Publishing, 2017

The Plot Whisperer by Martha Alderson, Adams Media, 2011

Verbalize by Damon Suede, Evil Mastermind LLC, 2018

Manufactured by Amazon.ca
Bolton, ON

18659644R00217